The Ballad of Katy O'Hare

From: *The Tales of the Spinward March*

Book Three

by David C. Winnie

Decembre 2019

To my Grandfather, Chester Amos Receveur
September 18, 1898- December 6, 1960
And to all the farmers who farmed to victory in two World Wars

Author's Foreword

"And so, it begins..."

These words, spoken in a haunting tone by Kosh from the television series "Babylon 5," (From the last episode of season one and at the beginning of each episode of season two) wrap up the story of *The Ballad of Katy O'Hare*. Many of my close friends and a few of my family know this was this first story I wrote, back in the late 1980's...very badly. I tried again a few years later after meeting my friend and mentor, J. R. Nakken. She is a woman of impeccable literary chops and speaks the truth, even if it hurts.

For a variety of reasons, I set this first story aside, not confident in my ability and certain no one would ever want to read my writing, anyway. Time passed and the stories in my head wouldn't fade. Indeed, they grew and changed, until I couldn't restrain them anymore. I wrote the first version of *Red Queen* and hesitantly gave it to J. R. She tore it apart, of course, as a good editor will. But she also said there was a story there, I just had to find it. Through months of work, I finally finished *RQ*. While trying to sell it, she asked me what was next. Dozens of ideas shot through my head, but she was enamored with Angkor Khan, who inhabited all of maybe two paragraphs and a few sentences in *RQ*. On her direction, I had an outline written a week later and eight months later I self-published *The Great Khan*. Your response to GK was tremendous, so *Red Queen* followed six months later.

And now you hold the third book in the series, which really was the first. Fans and friends have asked how long this series will last. Well, Book 4, *Descent* and Book 5, *Princes of Bastet* are already done, waiting for my fearless editor and me to finish all the work that goes into (what I hope you will find) some more good stories. I have begun Book 6 and have plans for a few more besides.

To the story teller, the dreamer and the timid artist who wants to tell the story burning in your brain: Get busy! The story is your story, that epic you daydream about on a lazy day. You only need find your Voice and write it down.

I look forward to reading it.

David C. Winnie
Everett, WA
June 2018

Credits:

Cover art: Bogdan Maksimovic

Galaxy, front cover top-left corner: NASA, STScI, ESA

Planet, back cover: Jonny Lindner

Book Cover Design: Creative Publishing Book Design
www.creativepublishingdesign.com

Author Photo: John McAlpine

The Ballad of Katy O'Hare

Prolog

Zurich, June 14th 3056

The long black car raced through the darkened streets of the government sector. These sorts of things always happened at night. All that was good and decent happened under the blazing glory of Sol, before throngs of cheering crowds. If the truth of what was happening tonight was ever disclosed, it would shake the Earth Union to its very foundation, perhaps crashing the whole Union and returning the world to its natural chaos.

Tenzing, son of Moi, Leader of the Earth Union Council, simply would not allow chaos to happen.

It galled Clementine Shurkorov that she hadn't seen the attack for what it until it was far too late to stop it. She had led the family after her father's mysterious death when Pomptenkin *exploded a dozen years ago. For all that time, she had achieved superb success. The family had enemies, yes, and those enemies would one day attack them. Preparations were made, the Shurkorov family would grind them down piecemeal and destroy them.*

She hadn't considered the government amongst those enemies.

She had fought well, using every means at her disposal to stop the collapse of the family's empire. But it was too many attacks from too many different directions. Tonight would be the conclusion of the Shurkorov family empire.

Today's battle was lost. Alternative plans had been set in motion. The family would have its revenge.

Some day.

Tenzing's insult was clear. The car stopped at the rear of Government House, outside the servant's entrance. A pair of soldiers were waiting, one taking her valise. She was escorted to the freight elevator; The Shurkorov matriarch wasn't even given the dignity of meeting Tenzing in his office. A small dingy meeting room sufficed, containing a battered metal desk and a pair of ancient folding chairs. She pulled a lace handkerchief from her sleeve and wiped one off before sitting.

She sat, upright, hands folded, waiting. Minutes later, the Great Leader himself entered, an aide carrying her valise. "You have the documents!" he demanded with no ceremony.

"Your security has been through my case," she stated. "You know it's all there." The case was dropped in front of her without ritual. She opened it and extracted the documents. This was it, all that was left of her father's empire, reduced to a half dozen sheets of paper.

"With my signature, all the assets of the Shurkorov Corporation transfer to the Earth Union, specifically to Tenzing, son of Moi," she stated. "In exchange, my family retains the yacht Volga, with seven cargo pods loaded to our specifications and permanent possession of a single rail fold ship."

"The first ten jumps of the rail fold ship are preprogramed," Tenzing said. "It will take you far from the Union. The next ten jumps will give you limited choices, each leading further from Earth. The twenty jumps are expected to send you a minimum of nine hundred fifty thousand light years away, far enough out on the Rim where it should be impractical for you to even consider returning. Where you go from there and what you do shall be your own business, save that your business never interferes with ours.

Rest assured, you will warn your descendants to avoid us at all costs. You and your family are under a death sentence for all time for your crimes against mine. Do you understand?"

Clementina stared at Tenzing for a long moment, then took the document and signed it. She spat on the contract and shoved it across the desk at the Leader. "If it takes ten thousand years," she swore, "the children of Alexis Shurkorov will have their revenge."

The trip to the spaceport was swift and silent. Her brother was waiting at the shuttle, annoying her. She had specifically ordered none of them travel together until they were all aboard Volga. Sergei typically did as he chose, but he was a valuable asset to Clementina.

For now.

"It is done then, yes?" his voice rumbled.

"Yes. We will go now, there is no reason to stay. The scientists are aboard and working already?" she asked.

"Yes, Sister," he responded. "We will head to the first jump-fold point as soon as you are aboard."

"Very well. Let's go."

The shuttle climbed swiftly into the night sky. The rail ship came into view within half an orbit. Already, her geneticists were hard at work examining the samples Earth had supplied. Each sample would be checked and checked again. Tenzing's son, Angkor, was a skilled geneticist. Without a doubt he had hidden something unwanted into the genetic material. Her scientists would check each line, every sequence. Any anomaly must be found and eliminated. The future of the Shurkorovs depended on it.

Fifteen hours later, the fold opening formed in open space, preparing to take the last of the Shurkorovs far out into the Rim. Clementina and Sergi watched the opening in time/space form.

"Sister, I have a question," said Sergi.

"Do they understand the nature of our research?"

Chapter 1

Spring 5132 A.D.
The Planet Saiphron IV

The red-tinged stalks of thassada rustled as the waves of an ocean. Not that Lars Thomas had ever seen an ocean. He had been born and raised on this world, Saiphron IV, under a pair of companion stars on the rim of the Milky Way.

The golden goddess sun, Saiphro, was life bringer to the system of five planets. Her companion star, Scorch, was a swollen red giant in the last throes of life. Two million years before, Scorch had consumed the last of his hydrogen and swelled, now burning what remained of his helium. In the expansion, the dying star engulfed his eight worlds, forever silenced the burgeoning civilizations.

The goddess sun escorted her five worlds around her tormented, dying brother for twelve orbits, before her path passed dangerously close to Scorch, burning every inch of her children's surfaces. Early settlers escaping the Terran Empire suffered terribly the first pass, three hundred years before, huddled in shelters. Emerging as Saiphron swung away from the red sun, the survivors rebuilt their towns and farms with screens that protected the citizens of the goddess's worlds from the demon red sun.

Those first settlers made a discovery that brought wealth and fame to the Saiphro System. During the three-month transit past the red sun, the burning and radiation renewed the soil. The first crop of thassada was inedible, filled with vile chemicals and sugars. But distillers of alcohols sought the red-black grains, creating exotic intoxicants demanded by nearly every species throughout known space. Each twelfth-year crop brought agents this far out on the Rim, eager to bid astounding prices for even the poorest of the granules.

Lars rode his air cycle to examine the northern fields. Two hundred years before, his great, great grandfather had ventured out at the Scorch's "night," when the spin of Saiphron IV faced the Goddess, rather than the red giant. A chemist by training and a farmer by vocation, he sowed various chemicals and salts across his baked fields. The theory was that by adding his concoctions during the renewal cycle, the size, speed and quantity of his crop would be far superior to his neighbors.

It was a tremendous success. Thomas Family thassada grain alcohol became the gold standard across civilization. The rest of the cycle, they worked as hard as the rest of the farmers of Saiphron to produce food grain. But for the vital first crop, Thomas Family were kings.

Today, Lars and his four sons were out examining the fields. It was important, this close to harvest, to watch the grain carefully. Harvest too soon, the sugars would be underdeveloped. Too late and fermentation would start before the distillers could work their magic. He dismounted his cycle and stripped a nearby stalk of its tufted grain. Rubbing it between his hands stripped away the husk,

Chapter 1

Spring 5132 A.D.
The Planet Saiphron IV

The red-tinged stalks of thassada rustled as the waves of an ocean. Not that Lars Thomas had ever seen an ocean. He had been born and raised on this world, Saiphron IV, under a pair of companion stars on the rim of the Milky Way.

The golden goddess sun, Saiphro, was life bringer to the system of five planets. Her companion star, Scorch, was a swollen red giant in the last throes of life. Two million years before, Scorch had consumed the last of his hydrogen and swelled, now burning what remained of his helium. In the expansion, the dying star engulfed his eight worlds, forever silenced the burgeoning civilizations.

The goddess sun escorted her five worlds around her tormented, dying brother for twelve orbits, before her path passed dangerously close to Scorch, burning every inch of her children's surfaces. Early settlers escaping the Terran Empire suffered terribly the first pass, three hundred years before, huddled in shelters. Emerging as Saiphron swung away from the red sun, the survivors rebuilt their towns and farms with screens that protected the citizens of the goddess's worlds from the demon red sun.

Those first settlers made a discovery that brought wealth and fame to the Saiphro System. During the three-month transit past the red sun, the burning and radiation renewed the soil. The first crop of thassada was inedible, filled with vile chemicals and sugars. But distillers of alcohols sought the red-black grains, creating exotic intoxicants demanded by nearly every species throughout known space. Each twelfth-year crop brought agents this far out on the Rim, eager to bid astounding prices for even the poorest of the granules.

Lars rode his air cycle to examine the northern fields. Two hundred years before, his great, great grandfather had ventured out at the Scorch's "night," when the spin of Saiphron IV faced the Goddess, rather than the red giant. A chemist by training and a farmer by vocation, he sowed various chemicals and salts across his baked fields. The theory was that by adding his concoctions during the renewal cycle, the size, speed and quantity of his crop would be far superior to his neighbors.

It was a tremendous success. Thomas Family thassada grain alcohol became the gold standard across civilization. The rest of the cycle, they worked as hard as the rest of the farmers of Saiphron to produce food grain. But for the vital first crop, Thomas Family were kings.

Today, Lars and his four sons were out examining the fields. It was important, this close to harvest, to watch the grain carefully. Harvest too soon, the sugars would be underdeveloped. Too late and fermentation would start before the distillers could work their magic. He dismounted his cycle and stripped a nearby stalk of its tufted grain. Rubbing it between his hands stripped away the husk, revealing the dull red kernel. Ah, the bouquet was perfect, earthy like a coffee bean with the slightest whiff of oaken smoke caused by the hard ultraviolet from Scorch. He placed a grain in his mouth and bit. The bitterness of the thin juice sprayed through his lips and into his mouth. Wicked, just the right bitter flavor and smoldering aftertaste.

He spat the vile taste from his mouth, then tossed the remaining grains high into the sky, calling out "Thank you, Goddess, for again leading through your accursed brother's realm of the damned and gifting us the bounty of his hellish lands." It was a silly ceremony, he knew. The quality of the grain he and his family would soon benefit was more due to dedicated science and carefully following a proven plan. But one should never grow too sure and ignore the gods who may or may not exist.

As he was turning to his air cycle, snowy brilliance lit the fields; his cycle became monochromic, silvery color with greying panels, the very air bleached to a painful glow. Crying out, Lars dropped to a knee and covered his eyes. The brightness faded and he tried to open his eyes but great spots danced through his vision and his orbs throbbed in pain.

Well, Mara, his wife, always had a poultice or soothing salve when he or the boys hurt themselves. Best he head back to the farmhouse and let her handle the problem. He tapped the comm on his cycle to call the boys and let them know he was heading back. Perhaps the flash hadn't affected them, in which case he wanted them to finish checking the crop. And if it had, he wanted them in, treated and back to work before sundown.

The comm wasn't working. Ridiculous. Jonas reported ten minutes ago, before advancing to the next field. The flash must have scrambled some of the god-rotting circuits. Well, that much more to do. He straddled his cycle and mashed the start button. It clicked once. Once again, and this time there was no response. The cycle released an acrid smell. He opened an access port and gasped. The battery was blackened, oozing its electrolyte onto the ground. Nearly every wire was charred and the motivator was smoking. The e motor spun just fine when he pushed the cycle experimentally. But any part that received power was either fused solid or burned.

The comm was melting like the cycle's battery. He removed it and wiped at the acid burn on his wrist. This confirmed his suspicion. Everything that was powered when the flash went off was now dead. Best he get back to the farmhouse and see how extensive the damage was.

He collected his hat and water bottle. While it should only be a two hour walk and he knew of three shelters between the houses and here, given the mystery of the power losses only made it prudent to carry the water. He extended the air cycle's aerial to its full extension, making it more visible. No telling for sure when he'd be back out to collect the ruined machine, so best to make it as visible as possible when the boys came out to collect it.

Lars made quick work of the journey, stopping only to check each shelter. They were unlocked, of course. Back in the early times, leaving a shelter unlocked for some poor soul caught in Scorch's deadly sunrise was a neighborly thing. Each underground shelter was equipped with food, water, medical supplies and a comm. Curiously, the communication devices appeared to work, though he couldn't contact the farmhouse. Apparently, several other farmers were in the same situation as he, caught in the open when the flash happened and now their powered vehicles no longer worked. Lars listened for his boys at each stop.

Good boys. Better to stay quiet and gather information than to broadcast their problems.

Leaving the final shelter a mile from his home, Lars collected the last piece of equipment common to all the shelters. He holstered the needle gun and slung the ancient shotgun over his shoulder. Neighbors were neighbors, his father had taught him. But if there was only room in a shelter to protect his and his own, better to save kin and sacrifice the unprepared neighbor.

The screen at the back door *scweeeeeed* at Lars' cautious approach, the muzzle of a slug thrower ominous in an inch-wide opening. "Husband, that best be you or some stranger is going to the next church social with a few extra holes." Mara's steady and practical tone had endured him to her ever since they'd met thirty years ago at the Scorch Harvest Festival. She wasn't the prettiest girl, but she worked twice her weight around the farm, raised the children to be hard working and respectful and still found time to sing in the church choir, although not very well.

"Woman, it's me and unless you want to have to carry me on your back to the festival, you might consider lowering that gun," he responded. The maw of the twin barrels disappeared, replaced by a stocky woman whose brown hair was streaked with silver. Mara wore a practical brown dress and work boots. She looked Lars up and down, then said, "Power's out, about three hours. Looks like you got some kinda flash burn going. Well, come on, let's get that dressed and get you fed."

At great expense, Lars' father had given the newlyweds an ancient iron farm stove for a wedding gift. Lars and Mara loved the way the old cooktop looked in their kitchen and found it practical as well. While cooking meals at the food station was swift and precise, Mara had spent the many years of their marriage learning to use the old stove. Holiday meals at the Thomas household were always events remembered and anticipated, as she would prepare each dish as their ancestors back on ancient Earth had, with the accompanying savory odors.

It was certainly earning its keep today. With no power, Mara had made bread and a pot of coffee. In a pot bubbling at the rear was hearty batch of *coompaht* in gravy. Lars poured himself a cup of coffee while Mara buttered his bread.

"Any sign of the boys?" he asked.

"Nah," she answered. "Given how far you sent them out, though, I suspect they'll be in within the hour."

A pair of screeches preceded short, tow headed creatures racing into the room. Both of his five-year-old daughters; Mika and

Mila, leapt onto their fathers lap, hugging and kissing. Mika sat back and pouted. "Da," she complained. "The telly stopped working."

"Yes," insisted her sister. "Just as *Barnkanaby Boop and His Marvelous Adventures* was starting." The girls began wriggling on his lap, singing "*Barnkanaby Boop leapt out of his coop and round and round started dancing. On his head went his boot and he hula'd his hoop and went out to go adventuring...*"

"You simply must fix the telly, Da," insisted one golden haired moppet. "Today is Friday and Friday is when he gets in a fix and we have to think hard all weekend how he ever gets out!"

"It seems, my precious gold mine, we have an adventure of our own right now, don't you think?" Lars kissed their noses and tickled their cheeks with his whiskers. "Here now, I heard the chickens scratching the dirt which tells me you've spent too much time waiting on the telly and not enough time on chores. So, scoot, scoot, scoot while Papa finishes his bread and fixes the power for Mama."

The girls hopped down, grabbed their buckets from the mud room and, squealing, ran to the barn to start their assignments.

Mara produced a small jar of refreshing cream; she was spreading it across his cheeks when they heard the cry, "Hallooooo, Thomas's?"

A tall, spindly fellow peddled into the yard on an old bicycle. Doctor Dander Palm, the new sector physician, dismounted his bike and leaned it against the porch. "Good morning!" the young man said. "Curious morning, what? Tell me, have you any power?"

"No, not since the bright flash," responded Lars.

The doctor squinted. "Flash burns," he muttered. "Haven't seen those since…" his voice trailed off.

"Come on, I'm trying my old generator in the barn, Doctor," Lars said, leading the young man along.

The machine was in a dark corner, under a dusty tarp. Lars hand cranked the motor several times before it went *chuff* and belched. He spun it once more; it responded with *chuff-chuff-chuff…BAM!* Chugging away merrily, it began spewing black, noxious smoke. The men fled the barn, choking, returning only when the atmosphere cleared. Lars twisted a screw and the machine idled down to an even purr.

"My word!" exclaimed Doctor Palm. "Is that an internal combustion motor?"

Lars nodded. "My grandfather bought it from a Solarian merchant when I was a child. We converted it to run on ethanol. Fortunately, we've had an abundance of chaff to convert and store in underground tanks." He flipped the circuit breakers; lights in the barn came on immediately, dim but useful. An adjustment to the engine and the lights brightened slightly. "Afraid, that's as good as it'll get," he said. "Let's see if the telly is working; maybe the news channel will know what's going on."

The girls were oddly quiet as their mother selected channel after channel of the vid. Each channel showed static and emitted uneven white noise. "There's nothing on the newsfeeds, Lars." Mara sounded frustrated.

"Try the government channels," suggested Doctor Palm.

The results changed. Shadowy figures and out of sync voices chattered and warbled from the wall-mounted vid. With suddenness, a clear image appeared, a haggard man in a smoke-filled office. "This is Administrator Jordan of Saiphron IV," the figure stated. "I am speaking to the ships attacking our world. Your first strike has destroyed our defenses. We have no means to resist. I am directing our police forces to assist you in any means you require. I am asking our citizens to lay down any weapons they have and comply with your orders as our new leaders. Please, we will give you what you require; all we ask is you stop the bombardment, particularly of our hospitals and habitations. We are at your mercy."

Chapter 2

The three adults sat in stunned silence as the message repeated itself continuously. The girls grew bored quickly, Mika tugging on her mother's dress asking, "Ma, can we watch cartoons now?"

Mara grabbed her child and hugged the protesting child to her chest. "No, honey, cartoons aren't on right now."

"Why?" wailed her sister. "I want to see cartoons. Now!" Both children began to cry.

"Mara, get them down to the shelter. Now," ordered Lars. "I'll monitor the comm until I hear from the boys. Go now." His wife nodded and gathered her confused children. "It's not Scorch season, Ma," whined the girls. "Why do we have to go down into the shelter?"

Mara's explanation was too low for the men to hear. Lars swept the dial from channel to channel on the comm, desperately scanning for word from his sons. Doctor Palm did the same with the vid. Images from the news channels began to appear. Grey and black ships, ugly, squared-off things with dark windows flew low over the cities of Saiphron IV. Gouts of fire spat from the war machines, exploding buildings, tearing up streets. Occasionally, smaller vessels could be seen racing even lower over the ground, seemingly firing indiscriminately. Humans would appear, fleeing for shelter. The machines chased them, firing webs and wrapping the terrified people, restrained where they fell.

Doctor Palm stood. "Lars, I have to go."

"Why?" Lars asked, "You can see it isn't safe."

"Overall of Saiphron IV, there are thirty thousand residents," Doctor Palm explained, "and fewer than one hundred doctors. With an attack like this," a bony forefinger pointed to the vid, "there are doubtlessly thousands in need of medical assistance. I can't stay here safe while there is suffering going on twenty miles away. Besides, they seem interested in captives, so I don't think they'll harm me."

"You could take shelter with us and go to the city once the raiders leave," argued Lars.

"I could," the doctor answered. "And hundreds could die because I did so." Dr. Dander Palm, newcomer to Saiphron IV, mounted his bicycle and peddled to his duty.

"Da, are you there?" A voice squawked over the shelter comm net. Lars grabbed the microphone and answered, "Yes, this is me. Who am I talking with?"

"It's me, Petr. Stephan is with me in shelter A-209," the speaker called. "Jonas just left shelter Z-006. He said he could see smoke and hear explosions coming from Port Arthur. He said he was going to go take a look and report back."

Lars swore. He needed his eldest son back here at the farmhouse helping plan their defense, rather than off making adventure. He thought for a moment, then asked, "Merc? Petr, where is your brother?"

The speaker hissed and spat for a long minute before Petr answered. "Merc is dead, Da." The boy's voice caught, then went on. "He was racing south when the flash struck. When I could see, I saw smoke from near where I last saw him. His air cycle dug in and exploded. He was thrown clear but landed on his head. His neck was broken, Da, there was nothing I could do."

Dear God, Merc, dead. Lars wanted to bury his head and cry. But he had the rest of his family to protect. "Listen, boys, gather weapons for yourself and every bit of ammunition you can carry from the shelters," he ordered. "Get back here as quickly as you can. Watch the skies, the raiders are using ships and drones to track us down. Stay out of sight as best you can, but get back here quickly, understand? I love you boys, now hurry!"

"We love you too, Da. Ma, too. We'll see you soon."

There were more than enough supplies in the shelter. But they could never have enough ammunition. He lifted the comm, calling Mara. He explained the situation quickly, omitting the information about Merc. There would be time for that later. "I'm going out to get as much ammunition as I can from the nearby shelters," he told her. "I'll call each time I return. Open the shelter door for no one until I tell you it's safe."

"I will, my love," Mara said. "Hurry back to us, Husband. We love you."

Petr and Stephan arrived the following morning, each lugging as much ammunition as he could carry. It was distributed throughout the outward facing rooms of the house. Lars had been busy as well, going around to the nearby shelters collecting weapons and food. It would probably be a futile gesture, he was sure. But any enemy who tried to harm his family was going to have a fight on their hands.

The girls were putting up better than Lars expected. Mara had explained about the bad people who were coming. Living in the shelter under the house was something the two youngsters had experience with. Every morning, they would clean themselves in the sanitation station, eat and dress, then race out to do their chores. Since Da had restricted the use of the generator to the evenings and then for only long enough to see what the bad people were doing, they amused themselves quietly in their room in the farmhouse during the day or studied the workbooks Ma supplied in the basement shelter.

The news on the vid was bad. After the first day, Administrator Jordan's message had been replaced by a hooded figure that hissed when it spoke. A translator spat its words. "We are the Sudahar Collective. The beings of this world are now our possessions. Humans are to present themselves for examination and disposition. If you comply, then no harm will come to you. Disobedience will be treated harshly. Any attack on Sudahar forces will result in punishment on the attackers and their families. You have no choice in these matters. Obey."

The message repeated itself over and over again on all the channels. Lars scanned up and down the channels; each showed the grey hooded figure repeating: "We are the Sudahar Collective…"

Jonas had not returned. Lars fought down the urge to sneak across the fields at night and go into Port Arthur to hunt for his son. Petr and Stephan, too young for war at fourteen and sixteen, would do the necessary farm chores early, then take up watch in the house's upper rooms, scanning the skies for the small drones or larger raider ships. Several times during the days that ensued they whistled; Mara would quickly lead the twins into the shelter while Lars and the boys watched the ball-shaped drones hum nearby.

The end came on the third day. Young Mila, always full of energy, had dressed and eaten ahead of her sister. She grabbed a bucket and ran for the coop to collect eggs. There was a curious whirring noise. She froze as a ball, nearly a foot and a half wide, swept in front of her from behind the barn. It consisted of grey and silver plates, patches of flashing lights and a triad of antennae spinning about its top. She screamed as a beam of green light scanned up and down her body. From the bottom of the hovering globe, a strand shot out and began wrapping around her tiny legs.

Lars bolted from the house on hearing her screams. She was too close to shoot the globe, so he swung his shotgun, beating the alien device to the ground. It sputtered and sparked, trying to bounce away. Once it had cleared his daughter, Lars fired both barrels of his gun into the dying machine.

He carried Mila into the house, tossing her to Mara down in the shelter. Both girls were screaming now as Mara snapped and broke the hardening web from the child's legs. "Quiet!" yelled Lars, then softer, "Quiet. Girls, you must be quiet. The bad people are here. You need to hide in the shelter where it is safe until Da and your brothers can scare them away." He and Mara shared a knowing look. She gripped a shotgun and nodded as Lars closed the hatch and covered it with a rug.

Outside he could hear a heavy thrum. He placed extra magazines in his pockets and chambered another round in his gun. Upstairs, he knew Petr and Stephan were positioning themselves, away from the windows, but close enough to see out.

Three of the round drones raced to and fro around the house in an irregular pattern. Lars recognized the ship; it was a gas giant collection shuttle, nearly big enough to fill the farmyard. It settled down ponderously, its landing gear hissing as they compressed, various jets of gas venting from its stern.

Behind him, a globe entered an upstairs window. Seconds later, one of the boys shot it and it came spinning out of the house, bouncing on the ground before climbing again and hovering unsteadily.

Doors on the front of the shuttle slid open. A pair of colossal humanoids exited, each wearing tight shorts and a red helmet. Several boxes grew from the giants' skin, wires and tubes connecting the various boxes. Between them, a pair of hooded figures stepped out. One called out in its odd, hissing voice. "You are now the property of the Sudahar Collective. You are ordered to present yourselves for inspection and disposition. If you choose to resist, you shall be subject to punishment. Come out now."

Lars stepped through the back door. He gripped his shotgun as he stared down the aliens. "I am Lars Thomas, and this is my home. I want you and your machines to leave us be and go away."

A grey, pebbled hand gestured with its three fingers from beneath the hooded robe and another of the globes crashed through a window. Another shotgun blast and it came careening back out. A second shot pelted one of the titans, who fell to a knee.

The hooded being raised a hand and pointed. A screeching howl froze Lars, followed by a dozen of large black and grey furred beasts exploding out of the ship. One leapt low and caught Lars in the chest. His weapon was wrenched from his hand and flung away. A massive clawed paw dug into his chest, pinning him to the ground. In his face was a roaring feline visage, long fangs dripping, and golden slitted eyes. Its fetid, rotted meat breath gagged him as the beast's heavy body held him down.

Four felines darted for the barn. The remaining seven flew across the farmyard. They crashed through the back door of his home or climbed the walls and entered the second story windows. He heard another gunshot, followed by an unholy wail. Moments later, the wall between two windows upstairs exploded outward, Petr's body falling amongst the debris. Another of the feline aliens, this one at least nine feet long, followed him out of the opening in the wall. It fell viciously on Lars' youngest son and began ripping the boy's belly open. Petr screamed as another beast joined the first, grabbing and ripping a leg away and scurrying a few yards away to eat. Petr's head turned to his fathers, his eyes pleading. A third feline took Petr's head in its mouth and he was gone.

Another of the giant cats strode out on all fours, dragging Stephan by the neck. He was quivering, still alive. Screams came from the house, followed by another round of gunfire. Lars recognized Mara's voice, her terrorized scream. His daughters were now mercifully silent. Lars saw them carried out by the neck and dumped unceremoniously on the ground. A pair of the balls floated over them and the girls were wrapped in a thick cocoon. Mara exited, dragged by her neck. The grey alien walked over and waved a rod over her prone form. He hissed and admonished the feline, striking it with his stick. Ears flattened against its head, the beast returned the hiss. A second blow and the protesting feline backed away from its kill. The grey figure spun on a heel and stomped back to the ship.

A globe appeared next to Lars. The feline over him held him down as the bounds surrounded his body. A pack of miniature felines, three-foot kittens, tumbled out of the ship. They chased one another across the farmyard, swatting and tumbling playfully, until one spotted Mara. It raced over and clamped its jaws around her head. The other kits saw their brother dragging the new toy and scrambled over to share his prize. Lars fainted from despair as they tore into Mara's body.

Chapter 3

The fetid odor of rotting manure and old straw woke Lars. His face was half buried in soft, moist filth. Trying to raise his head from the muck and clearing his throat only drew bile from his stomach. Retching, he struggled to an elbow, not wanting to vomit on himself.

"Easy, Laddie, let us help you." The voice was as gruff as the words were kind. Strong hands gripped his arms and lifted him, laying him over a steel rail. "O.K. Lad let 'er rip." The gorge in his stomach rose and rocketed from his mouth and nose. Even after his stomach was empty, Lars continued to gag and heave. In turn, his heaves turned to sobs at the memories of Mara and Petr's violent deaths. Stephan, Mila and Mika missing, in the hands of the mysterious Sudahar Collective. "There, there, Laddie, we're all in the same boat as it were," came the kind voice. "Suppose you stand now, give us all a wee bit more room."

Leaning against the steel rail, Lars looked over his cell. An animal stall, rough wooden walls to three sides, the steel gate behind him. A dozen filthy and nude men greeted him as Lars became aware of his own nudity.

"Wh-where are we?" he asked of a small, spry fellow, his beard and ring of hair crusted with the muck of their prison.

The little man had a quick smile. "I'm Angus Miller of Port Arthur. Our hosts have given us nothing but the finest suite at the

Port Arthur stockyards. Of course, it appears they overbooked a wee bit."

A glance through the barred gate confirmed what he had said. Across the muck-covered floor, another gated stall was visible through the gloom, with an indeterminate stall to either side into the darkness. Haunted faces peered back at Lars.

Angus became serious. "First things first. I need your name; spell it carefully." Lars followed the instructions, then understood as the little man tapped the wall and repeated the information in a low voice. "We have a fellah that managed to smuggle in a penknife and you don't want to know how. He's keeping track of every man who's come here and when they leave. So far, the average is three days. Some of us have been here for a week, most a lot less. They drag us out by a hundred and we haven't any idea what happens next."

"What about the women?" Lars asked. "They took my two daughters."

Angus shook his head. "We've seen nary a woman since we were captured. I watched them take my wife, but where…" He shook his head in resignation.

"I have…two sons left now," Lars swallowed. "Have they come through here yet? Their names are Stephan and Jonas." Another man tapped the wall and whispered hurriedly. Minutes later he reported, "Stephan arrived shortly before you did, but he was severely injured. We had just gotten his name when the Red Heads took him away. Jonas came in four days ago; he's still here."

"Jonas!" yelled Lars. "This is Da! Where are you, Boy?"

"Da!" came the distant reply. "I'm here! Where is Ma? Where are my brothers and sisters?"

The door at the end of the barn crashed open. Twenty red-helmeted giants raced in, swinging flexible rods that sparked and shocked wherever they contacted. Crowded in the stalls, men screamed as they were. A grey-robed lizard strode in. "The order has been silence. Who has broken this rule?" A hundred hands shot up.

"Here, ya bloody bastards!" "Me! It was me!" Yells and catcalls rang out, followed by handfuls of manure and straw. The lizard stepped out of the barn, shaking each foot as it cleared the muck, while the red helmeted giants began grabbing handfuls of men and boys, dragging them towards the open doors. There were cries of fear and screams of pain as the poles rained down on the hapless victims. Occasionally, there was the slap of a punch on bare skin, followed by more screams as some fought weakly against the giants.

The robed lizard leaned in the door. "It is fortunate the last lot had a higher than acceptable failure rate," it explained. "We are in need of thirty-seven more subjects. We shall examine this lot for the requirements. The remainder will be held until the next quota. The silence order remains in effect. Violation shall be met with great severity."

"Violation this, Asshole!" came the cry. A ball of feces landed near the lizard's feet. He pointed his rod toward a stall. A pair of the burly, helmeted giants opened the gate and extracted the perpetrator. He was a middle-aged man with a paunch. His cellmates were held back with the thin rods the other giants wielded. The prisoner was dragged kicking and struggling, forced to his knees before the lizard. "My compliments to the Feloids," the lizard stated. "Present this to them for their supper."

The gloom was replaced with darkness as their captors departed. There wasn't room to sit, much less lie down. Lars braced against the wall as he saw his fellow prisoners do and tried to sleep. Visions of the destruction of his family ran over and over through his head. He had failed. The first duty of the father and he had been swept aside as though he wasn't even there. Grief overwhelmed him, and tears flowed freely. Around him, other men either looked away or cried silently themselves.

Hours later, the main door opened again, with it the barest smell of green, spring air. A thin man wearing blue shorts and cap entered, pushing a cart. He stopped at each enclosure and handed in bread and bottles of water. There was no fighting; each man took his share and no more. When he reached Lars, the farmer saw it was Doctor Palm. "Dan!" Lars hissed.

The doctor's eyes widened, but he kept to his task. Barely moving his lips, he asked, "your boys?"

"Jonas is here, somewhere. The others…" Lars voiced trailed off.

The doctor passed a bowl of water. "Mara? The girls?"

"Mara is dead, killed by those farking b'tards!" Lars whispered, wanted to shout. "My precious daughters were bound like roasts to a fire and led off."

"Dear god, even the children," moaned the doctor. "Listen Lars, you are doomed. We're all doomed. You, your son, your cellmates, all doomed. You must accept you're going to die and most likely horribly. Your daughters…I don't want to tell you anything more than that their fate is worse than death. There are no heroes that will snatch us away, save us from our fate. The best you can do, the very best you can do, is to find a way to cut yourself open and let some of this muck you're standing in get into your bloodstream. With luck, you'll get an infection and be found unworthy. They'll kill you quicker that way. I've got to go; promise me you'll find a way to cut yourself." With that, he handed Lars his bread and water, and pushed his cart to the next stall.

The man to his right was named Benson. "He's right, you know," he said. "No one save the doc has left here and returned. Once you go out those doors, you're gone. They only keep Doc alive to feed us and to let them know when one of us has contracted the crud." He held up a gamey leg. "I'm almost infected enough," he explained. "Next time they call for volunteers, I'll go. He promises me a quick death and the felines won't eat a diseased body. Maybe I'll rot in an open field, maybe they'll recycle me. Either way, it's better than anything we've been told."

Lars thought long and hard. Saiphron IV was proud to have voted against joining the Empire. He himself had voted against it a dozen times, always proud to be a true pioneer in the strictest and most honorable sense. But now the folly of his pride struck him square in his face.

There would be no rescue. No Imperial dreadnaught was racing through otherspace to destroy the Sudahar Collective. No brave Imperial troops in their camouflaged armor mowing down the colossal cats or the red-helmeted giants.

No hope. None whatsoever.

He nudged Benson. "How do I cut myself to get the crud?" he asked. Benson put his hand on Lars' shoulder, understanding. "I'll do it myself. Lads, he's made the choice, hold him."

Several of Lars cellmates grabbed and held him firmly. Benson smiled and gave Lars a light kiss on the cheek, then knelt. Strong arms grabbed his right leg and lifted it from the muck. Lars screamed as Benson sunk his teeth deep into the skin at his ankle, twisting side to side to expose more raw flesh. He could feel his blood flowing freely from the wound. Benson eased his leg back into the putrid mud, arose and kissed Lars' cheek again.

"It's done, Brother," Angus said from nearby. "None of us could tell you to do it, the decision was yours. Now you are truly one of us, all damned, but we'll die on our own terms. Not theirs."

As expected, the doors slammed open three hours later. The twenty giants stormed in, their lashes forcing the prisoners away from the gates. The lizard strode in majestically and made an announcement, his voice hissing and metallic through the loudspeaker a giant held before it. "Sadly, for you all, none of the thirty-seven harvested last night were found acceptable. As such, we will be harvesting thirty-seven more to complete yesterday's quota, along with today's quota. As yesterday was such a disappointment, we have decided to harvest an extra twenty-five to ensure filling both quotas. Further, we will be taking from the most recent arrivals, assuming they have not contracted the odd condition your elders seem to be contracting. Begin the harvesting."

Screams and cries filled the barn as corral gates were opened and men were pulled from the pens. Many young boys were pulled out as well. The gate at Lars stall was opened, his arm was grabbed; he was jerked painfully away." "Jonas!" he called. "Jonas, this is Da! I've been taken!"

"Da!" His son's response was weaker than Lars' would have liked to hear. "I am coming, Da!" A Red Head shoved him back, but Jonas rushed the opening again. "That is my Da!" he cried. "If you are to harvest him, I demand to be harvested with him!"

"Familial loyalty!" the lizard exclaimed. "Fascinating behavior. I would not have expected this from such lower life forms. Very well, allow the child to be harvested with his father, if he wishes. It might even provide some entertainment to the process."

Shaking off the guards, Jonas hobbled over to his father, arms open wide. They embraced, weeping. "My mother?" Jonas asked. "My brothers and sisters?"

Lars shook his head. "Dead, all, except maybe your sisters. I just don't know. The last I saw, they had been cocooned by the drones and carried away. Your leg, what is wrong with your legs?"

Jonas turned his naked right leg toward his father. The ankle was festering and oozing puss, the whole leg red and swollen. A black streak led from his ankle to his groin. "I took the kiss the first day, Da," Jonas explained. "I was young and strong. There was no saying what they would do with the likes of me. Besides, the kiss was only a theory at that point. They needed test subjects to see that it would work. I am glad to see we had this one last chance, Da. I'm not going to survive the day."

Snapping lashes from their red-helmeted captors drove them outside the barn into the bright sunlight. Arms covered eyes unaccustomed to the goddess brilliance. Swift taps of the painful wands aligned them in a single line. Hoses, born by the ever-present red helmeted giants sprayed the muck and grime from their bodies. A small group of men in blue shorts and caps pushed buckets of soap up and down the line, using long handled brushes to scrub the soiled men, then the hoses performed again.

A few captives fell and were unable to get up. 12-foot hooks manned by the giants gaffed them and pulled them into carts, where necks were swiftly cut, and the wagons dragged off by more of the laborers. Jonas lost his balance because of his infected leg, but Lars grabbed his son and refused to let him fall.

He held Jonas ahead of him as they were marched across the stockyard, overseen by the hooks and wands of the giants. Jonas wobbled a few times. Lars, fearing the hooks, grabbed his son and kept him on his feet as they proceeded to the large barn at the end of the stockyard.

The wand tapped Lars, staggering him almost to his knees. He didn't dare fall to his knees, not this close. The red helmeted giants lined the walkway; behind them waited the blue-shorted slaves with their knives and carts. "Let go of the kid," one of the slaves yelled. "He has to enter on his own."

"It's all right, Da," said Jonas. "It's why I took the bite. This is the way it was meant to be." He leaned as close as possible. "Love ya, Da. I'll see you on the other side." He clapped his father on the shoulder and limped through the doors.

Five minutes later the door opened again, and Lars was shoved through. In another time, the room had served as a display ring, showing livestock. Around the sawdust floor were arranged booths. The dozen boxes were normally for agents looking to purchase stock. Tonight, a single box was occupied by five of the robed lizards, their hoods back. Their long heads and tiny eyes focused on Lars. The blue shorted slaves displayed him, turning him left and right, opening his mouth, examining his teeth. All the information was relayed to the lizards.

"It has the bite mark on its right hind leg," noted one lizard.

A slave examined it carefully. "It appears fresh, my Lord, no more than a few hours. No festering. A low-grade antibiotic will clean up any possible infection."

The lizards huddled for a moment. "Agreed, accepted," one announced. "Inoculate and store immediately. Next subject."

"Wait," demanded Lars. "What about my son? The man in here just ahead of me?"

A wand struck him firmly between the shoulders. Screaming, he fell to the floor, shaking. He saw a pool of blood next to his face, a streak of blood leading out the door to the right. "No," he whimpered. "Jonas…no."

Strong hands grabbed him and dragged him through the door on the left. A harness was wrapped around his chest, over his shoulders and fastened behind him. His head was fitted to a block. "There, there, calm down, boy," came a voice. "I'll be finished in a minute." Needles punctured his skin, injecting him with unknown, burning solutions. Feebly he cried out, "No, no. My family. Please, God, let me protect my family." The universe neither heard nor cared.

"O.K, just about finished," the voice continued. Lars felt a prick at the base of his skull. "This may sting a bit," the voice said. "Relax, it will all be over in a moment."

The prick pressed into his skull, a spike driven deeply into his brain. He jerked and tried to cry out as he felt wriggling, writhing filaments work through his head. With his vision greying around the edges, he gasped without sound as his body tingled. Every square inch of his skin burned, yet he couldn't flinch, couldn't scream.

"There now," the voice said. "That should feel better." A hand slapped him on the buttocks, releasing untold waves of pain.

"Okie-dokie, he's ready to ship," the unseen voice concluded.

Chapter 4

5244 A.D.

Eleven elders gathered on the main gallery of the great ship. Shortly after they stole the vessel, Augmentons built this room. It was similar to the Meditation Place back on the Home World. The Augmentons had found sand suitable to cover the floor. The eleven flat onyx stones had been brought on the journey in hopes that this shrine would be assembled.

The stones themselves came from their Home World. They were like the stones the elders would lie upon in the heat of its magnificent three suns. There they would discuss what important matters made up their day while the young would scamper about, hunting, playing and such. At night, the whole of the People would go below ground to stay warm and avoid the feral Hazzzrrack packs which roamed the world.

It was as it had been since the beginning. Doubtlessly it was the way it would remain until the end of times.

Then the visitors came.

They had been cast out of their people, they explained. Set adrift amongst the stars to die, their Home World so distant, it could not be seen on the darkest of nights. And they were dying. The marvels of their technologies could not stop their aging. Their ship, old when they departed, was deteriorating. They couldn't find a place suitable for colonization. Moreover, the radiations of otherspace had damaged them. Mating naturally created hideous, imperfect creatures. They would need new genetic material added to theirs or face extinction.

They offered much. Technology, something the Elders of the People had not considered, was there for the asking. Remarkable evolution for their bodies. They would no longer have to store heat throughout the day to survive the cold nights. Weapons that would not just defend them from the Hazzzrrack but make the giant cats their slaves.

The council argued that point. The visitors explained the concept of slavery and it was flatly rejected. The Hazzzrrack were dangerous, yes, but they were a free and proud people. In the end, the visitors agreed to make allies of the Hazzzrrack.

Medicines that would increase the lifespans of the People. More abundant and varied foodstuffs. Tools that made the most mundane tasks simpler and faster. More time for reflection and meditation, something of which the People never seemed to get enough.

The requests of the visitors were few. Since they were no longer fertile, they asked for a portion of the eggs produced each season to inject their own genetic material into, to regrow their number. The children, hybrids of both the visitors and the People, would be superior to both and enhance the future of both races.

The second request was for a plot of land to build their great factories needed to fulfill the plan. The People had never considered the *owning* of land. The visitors had explained this as well. This concept alone became the topic of discussion for days. While they never fully understood the idea, they agreed in principle to this thing the visitors were proposing. But for the visitors only.

The eldest of the visitors came down herself and stood amongst the Council. Due to time/space compression from the long journey through otherspace, while she appeared nearly two hundred years old, she was in conventional Terran time, nearly one thousand one hundred and fifty.

Clementina stood on a flat rock at the center of the council. While ancient, her voice remained clear and powerful. "Since the bastard Tenzing and his whelp, Angkor, stole my family's empire from us all these years ago, I have made it my single purpose to restore the Shurkorov name and to take back what was stolen," she declared. "If you agree to my plan, not only will you assist me, which I would consider no small favor, you will elevate the People to a position of wisdom and power, taking the night skies from our enemies and spreading the benefits of your contemplations and accumulated sagacity for all time.

I am to die soon. I will pass easier knowing that the future of your people and mine are assured."

The Council debated for months. They agreed to let the visitors have the land they sought and start building their machines. Hazzzrrack were captured and their experiments begun on the great cats. There was quite the uproar when the visitors brought the first tamed Feloid to Council. Yes, it strained at its instincts to tear into the People and devour them. But the great beast restrained its control and the meeting was a success.

Clementina was dying. The visitors were using every means at their considerable disposal, from chemical extraction of memory to microprobing select areas of her brain to extract information and experience. In this, their experiments with the Augmentons were useful. But to extract Clementina herself, her feelings, her experiences, the very essence of the matriarch leader they revered and feared, eluded them. And time for ancient body and brain was rapidly expiring. The visitors feared all she knew would soon be lost. The Council urgently requested she come before them one final time, for they sought to present her with a great gift.

A plinth sat in the center of the Council circle. Clementina lay upon it, encircled by the wires and tubes that kept her aged body alive. The First of the Council stood before her. "Mighty Clementina," he intoned, "the Council has chosen today to honor you in two ways. The first is to accept your generous offer. We, the Council, agree to make war as best we know, with the guidance of your children and the children of our race.

"The second is far more permanent, Great Clementina. Since our awakening half a million years ago, we have always saved a special place not just in our hearts, but in our very stones for the souls of the Great People who went before us. In this way, we not only kept them alive in our hearts, but in the stones as well, so in times of crisis, we could ask them for their wisdom. We have decided that you, Clementina Shurkorov, shall join the stones of our ancestors."

Before anyone could respond, he produced a knife and plunged it into her chest. The visitors gasped in horror, until they saw the smile on Clementina's face. A wide, toothy smile of victory. She raised her head and laughed, shook a bony fist at the sky and cried, "Fark you, Tenzing! For now, it is I who will defeat you!" Her arm fell, and her body slumped, lifeless as her soul drained into the stone that was the base of the plinth.

Back in orbit a thousand years later, the Council assembled on the meeting stones under the red giant, Scorch. An Ancestors Stone sat in the center of the circle. Today's meeting would be one of great importance.

They flattened themselves on the stones, reveling in the warmth of the red giant so close. At the appointed time, the First raised his head and announced, "Elder, we are assembled as you have ordered, and eagerly wait to receive your guidance."

A pillar of light rose from the black stone and formed into a youthful Clementina Shurkorov. "Good morning, Children," she said. "Whew, too bad my geneticists didn't spend just a bit more time on your appearance. Ugly little things aren't you?"

She greeted them the same way every time, laughing at the hybrid's development. She had hoped for so much more. They retained a bipedal form, but the joints were all wrong. Their faces looked human enough, save for their protruding muzzles. Worst of all was their inability to develop the warm-blooded trait. Pebbled grey skin made for better infrared absorption, but displayed a disfigured, ugly humanoid race. The First had asked about how they could make the People more aesthetically appealing to the Founder but would only receive shrugs. To do so would damage the strict balance between the two races and perhaps result in an uncontrollable cascade failure of the future hybrids. They would have to learn to put up with her insults.

"To business, then," Clementina ordered. "I assume the return fleet has been assembled per my orders?"

"Yes, Lady," responded the First. "This ship, while overly large, was stolen per plan and is being used to carry a bulk of the cargo. We have acquired another fifty ships, including fifteen warships, for the return journey. The number of Feloids to leave behind as sapper units have been bred and are being positioned as you ordered. We were able to infiltrate some of our more human appearing Augmentons within the local worlds. Finally, we have obtained the final number of female Terrans you ordered."

"The excess?" Clementina asked. "The unsuitable males, the drone Augmentons?"

"The disassembly of the drones has already started. Their biological components are being recycled as we speak. The Terran captives not directly needed for the operation of the ships or care of the cargo are likewise being broken down and fed to the recyclers. There was a minor issue on one world, Saiphron IV. The males captured there would open wounds on their extremities and allow them to infect. Thus, we harvested a two per cent less yield from that world. Nevertheless, from the other worlds we visited, we were able to achieve our harvesting goals."

"There is no problem with this infection spreading throughout the food supply?"

"No, Lady," said the First. "Antibiotics were administered to those not too badly infected. The rest were recycled and irradiated to eliminate any potential issues."

"Very well," Clementina said. "Please place my stone on the swiftest ship destined for home. Give the order to disperse the fleet per the plan. Release their agents at the appointed times and places. I shall see you all back on Home World.

Chapter 5

7234 A.D.

Since the dawn of time, when the first earth man struck down another with a rock, club or his bare hands, mankind has sought to preserve the imagery of its own inhumanity.

Archeologists unearthed and displayed pictures of the skeletal remains on the plateau of Masada, an entire city given to futilely sacrificing itself rather than surrendering to its Roman overlords.

Tintype images taken after the fierce struggle in Occident at Gettysburg where the soldiers lined up and fired away at each other until one side's courage failed, and they ran, leaving their dead and dying behind.

Blackened, frozen bodies in the Russian winter during retreat. Whether Buonaparte from Moscow or Hitler from Stalingrad, the dead were equally unrecognizable.

The mounds of dead and dying at Verdun, thousands dying each day for a few feet of advancement, only to fall back the next day.

The killing fields in the Khmer, Rhodesia, Somalia, and Syria. After a while, one would think mankind would grow numb to sheer numbers of the dead. Yet each generation sought to find even more horrific methods; demented, twisted techniques to kill with greater efficiency and cruelty.

When the killings ended, and the numbers had been counted, the victors would erect poignant memorials honoring the dead and proclaiming in anguished voices that *this horror would never happen again!*

Of course, some small incident always escalated, and the killing would begin again.

Commodore Katy O'Hare had only visited two of the monuments. The first was when she was a child. Reportedly, a great uncle had died in the Bougartd War. Her family voyaged to Bougartd to attend the dedication of the memorial monument the slave-Bougartd erected in the Capitol City, commemorating the thousands of Terrans believed to have been murdered by the previous regime during the long war with Terra. That Queen Annika Khan had killed billions in subduing the Bougartd was of no consequence. The victors always had, and always would, write the history books.

The Bougartd were extremely contrite for the murder of so many Terrans.

The second memorial Katy O'Hare attended was the yearly commemoration at Luna Prime. All cadets donned their EVA suits and marched past the remains of one sub-Lieutenant Bitsy Carmichael, Royal Army. Sub-Lieutenant Carmichael was still seated behind her console, her frozen hands gripping the edges, her hair streamed back and frozen from the rupture in her module on the original Luna One Base. Her eyes were milky and petrified, her mouth open either gasping her last breath or screaming. The cadets privately debated which, but it never mattered. Sub-Lieutenant Carmichael was surrounded by a low fence to keep the curious away, the last memory of the infamous day when the Chin attacked Luna One and destroyed the base. Each year, all the cadets of the Terran Imperial Academy marched past her remains on the open lunar plane and salute her, reading the plaque carefully placed at the base of her console.

DUTY

Duty. It was a word that fifty years later still haunted Commodore Katy O'Hare.

They were headed to a new battlefield, the Joeanmika system, a Wolfe Variable star. Nasty things, vomiting long, twisting streams of plasma and gas, intermixed with explosions of hard radiation. No being in its right mind would ever think of settling near such a schizophrenic star. But they made wonderful, frightening battlefields as Katy knew all too well. You could be sitting in plain sight, an enemy would charge up to fire on your seemingly helpless ship, only to find you had friends behind that gas cloud or perhaps you were riding the eddy of an intense radiation field which melted the enemy ship when it ventured into your trap. HUZZAH! Victory! Until your recently deceased victim's partner vessel would pop out from the plasma cloud that should have been closely monitored. And now, everyone was just as dead.

Katy stretched like a cat on her bunk. Even at sixty-five, she had what would best be described as a voluptuous body. As a career officer, she had always prided herself on being the most fit officer in the room. Thirty years after her disgrace, she still turned heads when she strolled the halls of a station, whether on duty or liberty.

They should be arriving soon. The uniform she wore was no longer the blue of a proud Naval Officer, but the brown of Salvage Services, the quasi-military scrounger established by Emperor Tory Russolov Khan, the eighteenth reincarnation of the Great Khan himself. The Empire had always taken great care to reuse and recycle any material it consumed, including the very bodies of its citizens. After a minor skirmish with the Rouden, the Khan had observed scavengers going through the battlefield, stealing valuable technology, leaving survivors to die if they had no means to pay for rescue and selling the remains of Imperial personnel for interment in the Queen's Necropolis in Giza.

Enraged, he hunted down the scavengers, then each of the scavenger's families and finally the home worlds of each scavenger. A dozen races, some friends of the Empire, found themselves incurring the wrath of an angered Khan. The message was clear; better to starve than defile the Khan's soldiers or steal the Khan's property.

Tory Khan ordered the establishment of the Salvage Fleet. Its task groups were to be the first units on the scene following battle. Their first mission was the rescue of any Imperial survivors and remains. The honored dead were sent to Terra for interment in the Queen's Necropolis.

The fleet would then set to work recovering the remnants and wreckage, packaging the scrap for transport to the Empire's forges.

The ships deemed repairable would be sent along to the shipyards and graving docks.

It was long, arduous work. Rarely was there any acclaim or reward.

Katy fastened her boots and donned an old knit sweater her grams had given her years ago. After the court martial, she had been stationed on Celebes, frozen companion world to Pluto. Grams had sent it along, urging her to stay warm. While Grams was decades gone, Katy could still smell the pastures of the Emerald Island, feel each loving stitch her grandmother had interwoven to create the sweater.

It was decidedly not uniform. Little in the Salvage Fleet was uniform. There was structure and discipline, of course. A fleet with its grave responsibility could hardly survive or accomplish its work otherwise. But the stiff, pretentious order and uniform had little place here.

Rank and file tended to adjust quickly, given the strong corps of petty officers and ratings the Council supplied. Newly commissioned officers or those, like Katy, dishonored and disgraced and sent to the Salvage Fleet for redemption, seemed to have more difficulty adjusting. In her task force, she gave each being limited time to adjust to their new role. But when the call to duty came after a fleet action, she expected each officer, petty officer and rating to do their job.

Failure would result in being dumped on the nearest planet, survivable or not.

She brushed her long red hair. When she served the Battle Fleet, she kept it short, regulation. Now that she no longer served the fleet, she had let it grow to nearly two feet in length. When working in an EVA suit, it took time and effort to tie her hair back, yet it was, for Katy O'Hare, as essential as Gram's sweater in declaring her independence, while serving the Law.

She settled back in her seat in the officer's mess with a mug of tea. When she first arrived on *Mary Kane,* she'd had all the automatic opening doors disabled. She told the crew it was to conserve energy. In reality, it was another step away from the sophistication and stuffiness of the Imperial Navy. Invariably too, at every meal and, if she waited long enough, there would be a thump at the door as some poor soul forgot the door wasn't sliding open. She'd listen to the creative cursing until the fool noticed the Commodore sipping her tea, a glint in her eye.

GOTCHA!

Breakfast this morning was bangers and toast. The mess was tiny, like all the compartments on *Mary Kane.* Officers sat elbow to elbow, rushing down their meals in silence. They were headed into a battlefield; everyone was tense. Katy preferred the mess this way before a mission. All of the officers present were scrolling through their pads, reviewing various bits of information and checking available supplies. New charts, some unfamiliar, had been secured to the bulkheads, designs of Imperial ships known to have been in the battle.

Katy sat at her place at the head of the table. Her meal appeared before her along with another mug of tea, over which their commodore studied her officers as she sliced her sausage and buttered her toast. This wasn't the first battlefield she would lead her small fleet into. The beings before her were as solid as any she had ever served in the Navy. More so than the officers she had served with on *Mikael Ender,* the destroyer crew which had led to her disgrace. This crew would follow her through an event horizon, howling all the way.

She ate swiftly, eager to start the mission. All the briefings had been handled, all the plans were place. *Mary Kane's* officers were burning off nervous, excited energy, waiting for the mission to start. Imperial Salvage expected the clean-up to last six months. Katy was determined to be finished in half of that.

She rose from her seat. By tradition, everyone rose with her. "All right then," she said, "Let's get to it." Nothing more needed to be said. This wasn't a crew that needed a pep talk.

The short stop in her cabin before she started work was routine, and necessary. The flask was in a side drawer of her desk, the bottle in her locker. She used the tiny silver funnel to fill the flask. It may only be a poor imitation of Glivenich, she thought, but it would do the job and besides, there was a special place in the afterworld for sinners who spilt even the poorest of whiskey. The capped flask went into the side pocket in Gram's sweater. She then poured herself precisely two fingers. One finger wasn't enough and more than two would indicate she might have a problem. Father had clearly had the problem, or at least what she chose to remember of him.

After the War of the Five Cities, humankind had come to realize the fragility of Terra. Emperor Janus Khan started the long, slow rebuild of Terra's ecology and the planet. His successors, save for the accursed Eight, continued clearing away the sins and pollutants. What could be salvaged was saved. What had gone extinct was left extinct as a lesson to the future generations.

Since ancient times, Glanearagh had been a fishing village in southwest Ireland. As the sea became barren, the hamlet painfully switched itself to heavy industry, further poisoning the land. When Angkor created the Empire and ordered his planet cleaned, Glanearagh became a heavy lift. Its traditional means of support was a poisoned ocean, while the means of survival they turned to was corrupting them as well.

The restoration of the country took centuries. While the planetary government cleansed the seas and restored the vast schools of sea life, the residents of Glanearagh bargained with the government and industry. Factories were removed, violated soils excavated, cleaned and returned. New industries were built, jobs became plentiful.

Michael, Katy's father, and his brother, Tom, took out a loan and built a fishing boat, one of the first in the village in centuries. The boat worked as a purse seiner for cod and a long line boat in the fierce winter weather when the elusive blue fish followed the cold waters northward.

The brothers were soon leaders and legends amongst the local fishermen. They had the newest vessel and financial backing. Recruiting crews was never an issue. The brother worked their crews hard and paid well. Their ship, the *Merry McCree,* was a tight, taut and clean running boat. Violations of any of the rules would find a hand beached the next time the boat came ashore.

After Katy turned seven, she went on her first cod trip. Katy was a brilliant student and her parents held high hopes for their daughter. Working the fishing boat where she could safely, Katy found herself part of a team. She observed her Uncle Tom closely, watched how he directed the crew while father drove the boat.

One rule the brothers held firmest. "No more than two fingers a drink." Mother explained the O'Hare family had a history of the trouble when it came to the devil whiskey. Mother herself was a teetotaler and a church-going woman. On occasion, Michael and Tom would both return from an arduous journey and stop at the bar after they had finished with the fishmongers. Eileen would give both the brothers holy hell when Michael came in drunk and give him even worse the next morning when the curse of the whiskey made him suffer. He would dutifully follow her to church and solemnly vow to never let the devil's blood touch his lips again. Back at the boat, they would sternly reprimand their crews and remind them of their order: "No more than two fingers."

The winter Katy was ten, the weather control rotated to a severe winter. To do otherwise would take the fragile ecosystem out of phase and create further havoc. Blue fish season came during the

January storms. For the first time, Tom and Michael had difficulty raising a crew. The weather would be too fierce, they were told, far too dangerous to fish the open ocean. As a result, the crew they took out was below their standard.

All was well for the first week. They reported the weather was tolerable and the fishing was excellent. The second week, everything changed. A fierce storm came rolling down from the artic, carrying record winds and high seas. Katy, her mother and all the families who had the boats out to sea that horrid evening kept close to the comms, listening to the distress cries and the words of encouragement the captains sent to one another. Father O'Callaghan broadcast a prayer and a blessing for the fleet just as the storm seemed to be at its worst.

As rapidly as it formed, the storm broke up. A total of thirty boats were lost, including *Merry McCree*. Fourteen fishermen, including Michael O'Hare, were rescued. When Eileen and Katy finally were reunited with Michael, he had ignored the two-finger rule and was roaring drunk.

Try as she might, Eileen could never get Michael to tell her of the last hours of the *Mary McCree* and of Tom's death. It was a well-known fact that there had been ample warning of the storm and Michael's reporting to the Board of Inquiry falling down drunk didn't help. The insurance company declined the claim for the loss of the boat.

Boat owners refused Michael's calls. Captains wouldn't hire him. That the lone survivor of a sinking was the Captain was unseemly enough. But a drunk. No one would hire a drunk.

Eileen finally kicked him out of the house. She sold the home and moved herself and Katy into a flat in town, took a good job at a factory assembling motivators for stardrives used throughout the Empire. But the hours were long, and she rarely had time for her daughter.

Katy buried her sorrow in her schoolwork. Occasionally, in a village the size of Glanearagh, she would see her father's former mates, who would suddenly cross the street to avoid her or find something quite amazing in the sky or a shop window. Women would pull their children away and *tsk-tsk* as Eileen and Katy walked by.

Three times, from the time mother cast father out, Katy saw her father. Each time, he was more haggard, dirtier…more *drunk* than she could imagine. The last time was the evening she was graduating from high school at fifteen. He stood outside the church and *hissed, hissed* as she marched by with her class. She blushed furiously as she entered the church, mortified he would have the audacity to attend. While she achieved top academic standing, the speeches, the honors and the scholarships went to less talented classmates. When her name was called, there was a low murmur as she strode across the sacristy to receive her diploma from the bishop. Only her mother applauded.

The class marched out of the church to joyful organ music. Outside, Michael, even drunker than before, whistled and clapped as his daughter passed.

It was too much. She whirled out of formation and stomped over. Katy swung her fist and knocked her drunk father on his ass and screamed, "You fuckin' sod! You've gone and fucked up everything else in my life, now you want to fuck this up to? Why don't you just go hang yourself or throw yourself into the sea?" Weeping, she ran home.

A month later, Michael O'Hare disappeared. A dory had been stolen from the docks. Neither were ever seen again.

As soon as Katy graduated, she joined the Navy. Her grades were outstanding, so she was sent straightaway to the Academy to become an officer.

Glanearagh would never again see the likes of Katy O'Hare.

Chapter 6

At nineteen, Ensign Katy O'Hare was commissioned into the Imperial Navy. Her first posting was as a supply officer on Euencladius Station. The job was boring and beneath her. Her fitness reports were outstanding, but she chafed for a grander job. Over and over again she filed for transfer to the various fleet throughout the Empire. Any job, as far from Terra as she could get.

She got her break during an inspection by one of the hundreds of captains, generals and admirals that often passed through Euencladius Station. A handsome squadron captain, Andre Lopez, preparing to depart for the Rim, complimented her on the neatness and accuracy of her section. "Easy enough when this is all I have to do," she grumbled. "But you should see what I could do if I was given half a chance at a real job instead of being an underused and undersexed bean counter on this nowhere station."

The curvy redhead had already caught the captain's eye. Her brassy attitude got her an invitation to dinner that night. Her twenty-year-old lusts got her into his bed. A week later she was on her way to the Rim. Six months later, after Lopez was realized the young ensign was more than a quick roll in the sheets and had real potential, he had her transferred to a fleet scout. Within six months, she was Sub-Lieutenant O'Hare and given command of the scout.

Her easy-going attitude belied her driven style. She demanded top performance from herself and her crew. A year later, when she was awarded a frigate, her entire scout crew volunteered to go with her. Three years later, her entire frigate crew nearly mutinied to accompany her when she was promoted to Captain of a destroyer. Five years later, Katy became the youngest Commodore in the Imperial Fleet history at thirty.

Commodore O'Hare and Balor Squadron (named for an Irish demon) became the scourge of the Imperial Border. They would sweep through a sector that was having trouble with pirates and raiders. Katy had learned her lessons well. Her squadron would attack not just the raiders, but then hunt down their bases and attack them as well. Imperial Justice grumbled, as there were few prisoners to try when Balor Squadron swept an area. Just what intelligence they could recover from data files and interrogations from the few survivors.

Balor Squadron was part of a fleet pursuing a Mousier Raider fleet. They departed otherspace on the edge of a Wolfe star in phase. Brilliant tendrils of gas and hard radiation blanketed the system. The smaller Mousier ships ducked and dodged around the branches of ship-melting death, disappearing into the glowing mists. Katy studied the maelstrom, trying to calculate how she could maneuver the squadron after the raiders.

"Commodore, Admiral Astor, Third Battle Fleet calling," came a call from the rear of the bridge. Katy nodded, and hologram of the Admiral appeared. He was an odious, fat old man, who never failed to remind his officers or anyone else in the room that his father had been *na-Khan,* the son of a near heir. While he carried no official royal title, in certain social circles, one was expected to acknowledge his near importance.

Katy found him an incompetent bore.

"O'Hare, why aren't you pursuing them?" thundered the two-foot-high round cartoon.

"Sir, we are analyzing the star and seeking the optimum pursuit angle to engage the enemy." Katy had long ago learned how to talk to idiots.

"Analyzing? ANALYZING!" roared the Admiral. "I don't see you analyzing. I see you acting with cowardice in the face of the enemy! I am ordering you, Commodore, to enter the system and drive the enemy out of the system so we can cut them to pieces." His holo stood even straighter, all of two-foot and one inch. "Am I clear, Commodore?"

"Yes sir," Katy conceded. "Balor Squadron…PURSUE!"

Without hesitation, her squadron followed *Mikael Ender* into the hellish system hiding the Mousier Raiders. Two raiders were destroyed in short order. Three turned in panic and collided with invisible gas belts and melted.

The game of cat and mouse began. The smaller, more maneuverable raiders ducked and scuttled about. The destroyers moved cautiously, their sensors mapping the eddies and currents of the ever-changing gas cloud. They tracked the raiders and set ambushes, but not without casualties. *Tedeore Ruiz* failed to twist correctly on a turn. A spike of gas penetrated the hull and the ship was immolated.

Mikael Ender was pursuing a pair of raiders. Eddie Blasini, her First Officer, sweated as he stared at the sensor readouts, the twists in the plasma were growing narrower and narrower. "Commodore," he pleaded. "The passage is too close. Let these two go. We have to get out of here."

"Enough, Commander," she coolly replied. "We'll squeeze through just fine. Weapons?"

"Thirty seconds until we're in range, sir," came the response.

The ship shuddered. The bridge plunged into darkness, save for emergency lights and half the consoles. "Eddy current to starboard," reported the sensor operator. "We just tagged it with the starboard nacelle."

"Conn, Engineering, what the hell was that!" The report over the tannoy was angry.

"Engineering, this is the Captain," Katy snarled. "Commander Wiebe, pay attention to my engines."

"Engines hell," Wiebe roared back. "That hit just took out the starboard engine. We're venting atmosphere and plasma right now. I just lost twenty good men and women!"

"Seal the damn chamber then and give me power, Commander!" Katy kept her voice firm. "I have two targets in range in…Weapons?"

"Fifteen seconds, Commodore."

The Engineer continued to rage, so Katy cut the comm. Fifteen seconds later, the *Mikael Ender's* meson rifle fired a dozen rounds, destroying the two raiders.

"Come about to port, find me the next target," ordered Commodore O'Hare.

"Commodore, we're damaged," said Commander Blasini. "Badly damaged. We need to withdraw and repair the ship."

"Blasini, there are half a dozen raiders out there." Katy said. "We're going to get after them.

"Commodore, I must insist."

Katy heard a click and felt the pressure of Commander Blasini's sidearm at her temple. "Commander, you're playing a dangerous game here," she warned.

"I'm saving my ship, Commodore," he said. "Now, order us to withdraw."

"No."

She could feel the weapon quiver slightly. She had him. "Commander Wiebe, report to the bridge." Blasini ordered.

Moments later, the short, wide engineering officer entered the bridge. He took in the bridge crew frozen at their stations and Blasini with his side arm at the Commodore's head. He made his decision. "Commodore, are you maneuvering us away from this damn star?"

"No."

"Then I have no choice. Commander Blasini, I acknowledge that the Commodore is incompetent to command the *Mikael Ender*. I support your relieving her of command," he stated. "Commodore, at this point, I am required to place you under arrest and confine you to your quarters."

"Oh?" replied Katy. "You honestly believe it's that easy. 'Commodore, I'm scared shitless, so if you won't run away from danger, we're going to try and take over.' You fools, this is both mutiny and cowardice before the enemy. The sentence, by regulations, is spacing. If any of you other officers go along with this, you will be joining these cowards in the airlock."

"There will be no spacing," said Blasini. He picked up a microphone and toggled the tannoy. "Attention, crew of the *Mikael Ender,* this is Commander Blasini. I have relieved Commodore O'Hare of command. We are seriously damaged and need to withdraw for repairs. Commander Wiebe is in agreement with me. We ask you all continue to do your duty while we move the ship to safety. Security Chief Chambers, to the bridge to escort the Commodore to her quarters."

Moments later, five armored security men entered the bridge, weapons drawn. They circled the bridge, aiming their weapons at every person on the bridge, shifting their targets quickly. Security Chief Chambers entered the room, a massive black man in heavily scarred armor. "Commodore, Commanders," he said, "I take it the situation is under control?"

"Yes, yes, take her away," snapped Wiebe. "We have work to do."

"Commodore?" Chambers asked.

"You know what to do, Chief," she ordered.

"Yes, Ma'am." His rifle came up and butt stroked Commander Blasini in the back of the head. The weapon's swing ended in a point at Wiebe's ample belly. His boot lay on Blasini's neck. At a motion from his free hand, troopers secured the prisoners and pulled them to their feet. "Orders, Ma'am?"

"Take these two the shuttle bay." She took the microphone. "Crew of the *Mikael Ender,* the mutiny has been put down. Imperial Intelligence to the bridge. All hands are ordered to remain at their posts until released."

The petite Imperial Intelligence agent, Tan Choi, arrived. Dressed in black, her long dark hair was in a tight ponytail. "Commodore," she said.

"Tan, I want you to scan the entire crew," Katy ordered. "If these two officers were cowardly enough to attempt mutiny, there must be others."

"They will resist," the agent said. "There is the Right of Privacy."

"We are in a combat situation," said Katy. "I don't have time for such niceties. Find the traitors, report them to security, and assemble them in the shuttle bay."

She extended her hand to the gauntleted hand of Chief Chambers. "Thanks again, Chief," she said. "What's the count up to now?"

"In the last five years or the last twenty?" The chief's laugh was a belly rumble. "Commodore, I've told you a dozen times, you keep sticking your head in the lion's mouth, I'll keep pulling it out."

"Let's get this done then, Chief," she ordered. "I have a battle to finish."

While *Mikael Ender* maneuvered through the plasma clouds hunting the raiders, the roundup of traitors was finished swiftly. Starting on the bridge, Tan pointed at three officers. The security guards cuffed and led them away. Within the hour, she had secured thirty- seven officers and ratings who failed her scan. They were assembled in the shuttle bay, unsure of their future. They found out soon enough.

Katy appeared in the entrance. She read from a pad. "You have all been found guilty of treason and making of mutiny, with the added enhancement of occurring in the time of battle, which adds the charges of cowardice. According to the Laws of Angkor Khan and Naval regulations, the sentence is death by spacing. There is no appeal." She stepped back, and the airlock closed. Before anyone in the shuttle bay could react, the external door opened, sucking them all into space.

Katy swung by her quarters and had two fingers. She then returned to the bridge. There was a battle to be won.

A week later, the nine remaining ships of Balor Squadron, led by *Mikael Ender,* escorted the last raider from the plasma and radiation surrounding the Wolfe star. The raider was halted before the Admiral Astor's battle cruiser. Furious, Admiral Astor ignored the raider and departed immediately for Timor Station, leaving Balor Squadron with its captive. As the last of the battle line departed,

Katy ordered the raider destroyed and set course for the nearest naval yard for repairs.

Her reward was to be arrested by the Admiral and charged with treason and disobeying orders. The charges were ludicrous, and she was certain of acquittal. The night before the court martial her old friend and sponsor, Admiral Lopez, paid her a visit at Whitechapel Station in orbit over Terra. They supped, then took a whiskey, gazing out the windows overlooking the night lights of Terra.

"Katy, you'll need to plead guilty," Andre told her.

"The charges have no basis," Katie argued. "When the court hears the facts, they'll not only acquit me, they'll probably give me another damned medal."

"You don't seem to understand what's happening here," Andre said, "Admiral Astor is a moron. But he is a minor Royal and you embarrassed him. Not because you followed his orders and entered the gas cloud. But instead of driving the enemy out to where his fleet could destroy the raiders, you defeated them yourself. This embarrassed him that a squadron of destroyers accomplished what he couldn't with a whole Battle Fleet. Further, word of the mutiny on your ship has reached his ear and he intends to use it against you as a demonstration of your incompetence. You'll be stripped of your rank and status at best, executed at worst. There is an option:

"The Khan despises her cousin. She can't order him not to court martial you, but if you plead guilty, she'll pardon you and appoint you to the Rescue and Salvage Service in your same capacity."

"So my choice is prison or transformation to a cosmic garbage collector."

"Your choice, my love, is to serve the Empire and the Law you swore an oath to, or execution," Andre replied.

The court martial wasn't the show Admiral Astor wanted. Katy, in her full uniform including medals and decorations, quietly pleaded guilty to all the charges. Admiral Astor, denied his chance to perform in front of the Court board, roared and raged, insisting that as the son of a *na-Khan,* it was his duty to present evidence against this treasonous officer. The board, fully aware of the bombastic Admiral and his reputation, denied his demands.

As a Flag Officer sentenced to death, Katy was entitled to an appeal before the Khan. She was dressed in an orange jumpsuit, denoting her prisoner status, cuffed and shackled, shuffled into the Grand Hall and led by Imperial Guards to the foot of the Khan's throne, where she knelt. As the Empress entered, one of her guards gently placed his boot on the back of her head and forced it to the tiles.

"Let her up," the voice was high, but rich. "Let me see her face."

The Empress was spectacular. Wearing a simple, elegant gown, her slender, coffee-colored fingers lightly gripped Katy's chin, turning the prisoner's face side to side. Long, angled planes formed her face, emerald sloe eyes studied Katy with compassion.

"You are attractive, Katy O'Hare," commented the Empress.

"Thank you, Ma'am," Katy said. "I must say, you are stunning."

"Ah, but I was designed this way," the Empress sounded a bit sad. "You, on the other hand, have an inner beauty which comes from a lifetime of experience I can only imagine. Please, Katy, look at the floor beneath you."

Katy looked down. The tile beneath her appeared to be a large pool of blood, though hardened rather than fluid.

"Dohlman!" called the Empress. A primly dressed holo appeared before her. "I forget," she confessed. "Is this the blood let from Angkor's brother Suishin or is this where Annika murdered the pretender?"

"The blood is from Mi Sing ne-Khan, Regent of the Empire between Emperor Robert De L'Orange Khan and Queen Annika Raudona Russolov Khan, the fourteenth and fifteenth reincarnations of our founder, Angkor Khan," reported the holo. "After she cut his throat, she ordered him bled out, then the bloodstain to be preserved as a warning to all who appear before the Khan for justice. Normally, we keep it covered with a nice rug."

Thirty years later, in her cabin aboard the *Mary Kane,* Katy O'Hare lifted two fingers of the *faux* Glivenich to her long-departed lover. "Here's to us, Andre. War hero and cosmic garbage collector." She quaffed the drink and slammed the glass on her desk. They would be reentering normal space in minutes; she had work to do.

Chapter 7

A guard slid the door open as Katy approached the bridge of the *Mary Kane*. Katy insisted on function over protocol. None of the twenty crewmen working in the nerve center of the salvage ship leaped from their seats as would be expected even on the smallest Imperial scout ship. One or two looked up as the guard announced, "Commodore on the bridge." But there was a job to do and Katy, raised on her father's fishing boat, demanded sweat over salutes.

She settled in her workstation overlooking the holo projector. While *Mary Kane's* bridge was ringed with windows, a majority of the running the rescue and salvage would be done via sensors and projections on the main holo. Aft of the bridge was an observation tower, should Katy decide to get a visual on an operation. Unlike a combat vessel, the Captain's station wasn't located at the center of the bridge. Rather, a circle of ten workstations surrounded a hologram projector with Katy sitting at the five o'clock position. Ten other workstations circled the central area, facing outward, monitoring ship systems. The lights were kept low to save energy and make the displays easier to view.

"Tactical," ordered Katy. The holo swirled and formed the Wolfe star system where the battle had happened. The fleet was in the process of arranging itself around the target with green chevrons indicating her ships. Cyan circles moved haphazard orbits. These were the largest of the debris the sensors could detect. It could be portions of ships, clouds of gas…or enemy vessels lying in wait for her small fleet to attack. Hence, fighters and scouts would sweep the system before the fleet would set to work.

The heavy tugs had already released their ten scouts, along with *Mary Kane's* two.

"Stellar cartography?" asked Katy.

Jayne Conner, the ship's astrophysicist, punched a few keys. The display changed, showing a smaller orange star. "Ladies and gentle beings, I give you Joeanmika 46, a young Wolfe star currently in remission, although there are still several plasma clouds and heavy radiation belts in system to contend with. Joeanmika 46 has stopped ejecting stellar material; I believe it has entered passive stage for twelve standard years. More than enough time for us to accomplish our mission. There are seven proto planets, but none are habitable. There is a pair gas giants, so *Solarius Maru* will have a resource to mine and produce fuel for the fleet."

"Signals?"

Boston Xillia reported, "Hard to say exactly, Commodore, until we enter real space, but we are picking up numerous disaster beacons, which indicate larger ships and faint emergency beacons that could be escape pods or individual signals. We can get you a better idea once we exit otherspace."

"Captain-sister 93," called the Commodore. The holo reformed to a yellow-green Vinithri. Her mandibles worked and emoted scent into her translator. "Commodore Katy O'Hare. The honor is to serve. Imperial carrier *Valiant* stands by for orders."

"Your service honors us, Captain-sister," acknowledged the Commodore. "All ships prepare to exit otherspace. *Valiant*, launch all fighters on entering real space. Sweep the system for expended weapons. Frigate group 543, establish a defensive perimeter. Monitor all signals, watch for any active enemy vessels. All scouts begin search and analysis. Until we have a picture of what we have here, attempt no rescues. They've survived a week, a few hours more won't make a difference.

"*Solarius Maru,* select which gas giant is most viable and start producing fuel. All remaining ships start tracking signals and interfacing with *Mary Kane*. All ships acknowledge."

Reports poured in from every vessel. First Officer Jhon Bosley stood and saluted Katy. "The fleet stands ready, Commodore."

"Execute."

At the prow of each vessel, from the mighty *Valiant* to the frigates, tachyon beams reached out and gripped at the fabric of space. At the sub-atomic level, reality separated, creating an opening between otherspace and real space. Earlier versions of the otherspace generators used massive energies that tore the fabric. The modern version opened space only as far as needed and closed it cleanly behind each ship as it emerged. Without hesitation, a mixed bag of ancient *Scimitar* and *Buccaneer* fighters, all hundreds of years old but lovingly rebuilt and maintained, exploded from the launch tubes of the *Valiant.* The forty ships raced through the system, examining every manufactured item visually and firing on any object that remotely resembled an unexploded weapon. They also sighted dozens of rescue pods, reporting their position. Their mission was to make the system safe.

The scouts flew behind the protective screen of the fighters, sensors checking each beacon. There were three full vessels with holes in them, appearing dead. Hundreds of ship parts tumbled in erratic orbits. Katy watched with pride at her pilots' skills, dodging tumbling parts, finding and firing away at drifting weapons and marking more than a dozen rescue pods and dead shuttles in the maelstrom of debris. No rookies in her fleet, each fighter pilot had been deemed too old for continued front line service with the Fleet. Katy had eagerly accepted them for service in her command and now watched them perform their mission with élan and pride. *"Getting older doesn't mean you can't do the job you love and do it well,"* she thought.

Captain-Doctor Ho-Bar of the hospital ship *Tranquility* tapped on the Commodore's door. He found Katy sitting at her desk with exactly two fingers of Glivenich, a second glass waiting on the table. "Gah," spat Ho-Bar. "One day, I must bring you some kasavassa. Much more flavorful than this swill."

"That'd be wonderful, save for the strychnine issue," Katy answered dryly. Ho-Bar was from Zernon, one of the first worlds on the edge of the empire where the entire population had been designed, then inhabited the planet. Zernonites were tall, powerful and attractive, save for a few idiosyncrasies in their biology. Such as strychnine replacing many of their blood sugars, rendering most of their food and drink poisonous to other Terrans.

"Are *Mercy* and *Repose* ready for survivors?" Katy asked.

"They are," sighed Ho-Bar. "As is *Respite*. As hopeful as I am for the survivors, I fear *Respite* will have more work." *Respite* was the mortuary ship. His primary role would be to identify all the remains and prepare them for returning to their Home Worlds, as well as taking a sample from each for interment in the Queen's Necropolis on Terra.

"At least we'll have remains to return to the families," Katy said. She stared at her drink for a long moment, the quaffed it down, at once reaching again for the bottle.

Ho-Bar placed his hand on the bottle. "You and I have talked about this," he said. "We agreed two fingers. No more."

"I'm off duty now, Doctor."

"As our leader, you're never off duty," said Ho-bar, "and you've already had more than that."

Katy scoffed. "You just saw me have my drink."

Almost too quick to see, he dipped his hand in her sweater pocket and came out with her flask. He shook it and the last bit sloshed in the bottom, was promptly tipped into his mouth. "I'd say this holds a great deal more than your agreed allotment."

"You know I face pressure all day," argued Katy. "A nip here and there keeps me focused."

"This is more than a nip or two," the doctor lectured. "Katy, we've talked about this. You have a history of alcoholism in your family…"

"That history died with my father!" yelled Katy, pounding her fist on her desk.

"That history likely passed to you," Ho-bar said. "You may be able to control from time to time, but we've both seen you get out of control."

"This is not one of those times." She took her flask from the doctor. "I have the situation well in hand Doctor. If I suspect a problem, I will of course notify you. In the meantime, I suggest you return to *Tranquility* and stand by for survivors. Good evening, Doctor."

"Katy, I…"

"I said good evening, Doctor." Katy keyed her computer and studied the screen. With her free hand, she poured another drink.

Captain-Sister 93 reported. The outer third of the system was clear enough to send in the recovery and survey teams. Her fighters would continue into the middle third.

"However, there are still heavy clouds of plasma closer to the Wolfe star which makes it too hazardous to operate my fighters, "Captain-Sister 93 relayed. "I could order them in, but I fear we would be forced to rescue injured pilots and damaged fighters. Given their heartier construction and shielding, I recommend we use scouts to survey the zone closest to the sun."

"Agreed. *Mary Kane*, *Kinterkae* and *Lisalui* scouts to survey the inner third," Katy ordered. "All ships launch cutters and shuttles begin to start the recovery operation. Priority on personal beacons for now, but if you come across a life pod, grapple and get it to a hospital ship immediately."

The shuttle from the frigate *Fiacius* had been assigned an area that turned out to have multiple personal beacons. The pilot maneuvered close to the first three targets. Tragically, in each instance the life support had expired, or the suit had been damaged; the occupant was dead.

Dennis Fix would lead members of his platoon out to recover victims. When they found a dead body, they attached it to the outer hull for transport to *Respite* for identification and disposition.

Having secured three bodies already was discouraging. Granted, it was nearly two weeks after the battle, but the survival suits were designed to last much longer. Perhaps all the radiation had something to do with it.

They were approaching the fourth casualty. Fix, a hundred yards away, saw its arms and legs moving slightly. "Privates Hane, Boyer, with me," ordered their sergeant. They clipped tethers to the hull of the scout and used suit jets to maneuver to the weak survivor. Fix arrived first, clamping his arms around the chest and pressing his faceplate against the victim's. He was assuming the suit still had an atmosphere; the direct contact should transmit his words. "Hey, hey, relax, Buddy," he shouted. "I'm Sergeant Fix and we're here to rescue you. Just relax and let us do the work, O. K.?" The victim's visor was opaque, so Fix wasn't sure if he understood, but his struggling slowed. While the hoist pulled them to the shuttle, Private Boyer began first aid. "Fark!" he snarled, "this shygyt for brains got his suit on wrong. I can't get a revealon line connected; he's got something blocking the port."

"So, we get him in the airlock and get his helmet off and start the line straight to his carotid artery," Sergeant Fix responded. Private Hane positioned himself feet first toward the shuttle. He noted the victim was unusually large, so he adjusted his grip, cushioning the blow with his legs when the group reached the small ship. It was a tricky, but necessary maneuver. The mass of the four beings moving swiftly could have caused significant injury if allowed to slam into the hull. Hane's training kicked in and he absorbed the blow with a grunt and rotated the four beings into the open airlock.

The victim's bulk threw off Hane's carefully practiced brake and spin maneuver. Instead of a gentle landing inside the airlock, with the victim lying on the floor and the soldiers in position to render aide, they tumbled about, bouncing off the inner walls. The corpsman watched through the inner door anxiously for the writhing mass to secure the outer door. Hane spied the switch near his boot, made a desperate kick. The outer door slammed closed and atmosphere flooded the chamber.

Lights flashed green, the door into the shuttle snapped open. Privates Boyer and Hane moved out of the way, giving the charging corpsman more room to work.

Fix, helmet unclipped, took a deep breath of the ship's fresher air. He unclipped the survivor's helmet and removed it. As the helmet cleared the being's red head, it gripped the corpsman by the throat and threw him against the far bulkhead, hitting with a sickening *crunch* and slumped messily to the floor. The alien reached with its other hand and grabbed the back of Sergeant Fix's helmet. Private Hane leaped across the airlock, catching a boot in his chest, flying back and hitting Private Boyer, who was trying to re-enter the airlock.

Sergeant Fix's knife appeared in his hand and began stabbing the huge arm of the augmented warrior, gripping its head, while twisting his body trying to break its grip. The alien's helmet bounced away, revealing a red humanoid head with no features; no nose, no eyes, no ears, no mouth. Fix ended up on top of the creature, face to featureless face. Its unwounded arm grabbed at Fix's helmet again and the Sergeant tried twisting away once more, stabbing wildly. Crimson blood sprayed from the alien's wounded arm as it grappled and gained purchase, flipping Fix onto his back atop its giant body. The other, uninjured arm wrapped around the sergeant's chest in an iron grip, while the bleeding arm reached up, grasped Fix under his chin and began pulling.

"Blow the hatch!" Fix ordered through gritted teeth. "Now, do it, blow the fracking hatch!" His voice croaked away as his head was bent backwards.

Hane slapped the control, the inner hatch to the airlock closed. "NO!" screamed Private Boyer. "Open the hatch you glarpshite! Sarge, we're on the way."

"Blow the hatch," gagged Fix. "Dear gods, hurry, blow the ha…" with a squeal, then a sickening crunch, as his bent head reached the point of no return. Arterial blood shot from his neck as his head left its body.

Private Hane hit the external hatch release. The head of Sergeant Dennis Fix, Imperial Army, flew out, followed closely by a frozen cloud of blood, the alien and the dead corpsman.

Boyer sunk to the floor. "By all that's unholy," he gasped. "What the frack was that?"

Chapter 8

Disaster calls rang out from the entire system. Nearly every ship ordered to collect survivors reported being attacked by aliens in Imperial survival suits. Ten soldiers were confirmed dead. Two ships, a cutter and a shuttle, failed to respond to hails. The cutter's engines glowed, and the ship arced toward the frigate *Damalie*. Too late, the frigate fired on its own cutter. The cutter exploded; its fragments ripped through the slender warship. *Damalie* rolled out of attitude, escape pods racing away from the dying warship. It exploded, adding to the carnage of the system.

The other non-responsive ship, the shuttle, drifted off axis, dead.

"What in the hell?" swore Katy. "Comm, fleet wide. Break off rescue of individuals. We'll figure that out later. If a suit powers up and heads towards any ship, destroy it. Gather the rescue pods. Frigates *Hecate, Carlotta* and *Garnuaschil*, establish a quarantine for the pods. We'll check them one by one for Terrans and citizens. We'll deal with the aliens when we figure what we're dealing with."

"Tan!" the diminutive Imperial Intelligence sprinted to the Commodore and braced. "What is happenings here?" demanded Katy, "Who did the fleet fight here? What species are we dealing with?"

"I'm sure I don't know, Commodore," said the black clad agent. "I received the same information you did. I can only speculate there was information not made available when the orders were issued."

"You speculate," said Katy. "You speculate?" She pointed to the hologram, the headless body of a soldier drifting through space. "And what would your finely tuned senses speculate that was? I want answers. Get on the farking comm, contact your motherless supervisor and get me answers!"

The wedge-shaped scout was nearly in the star's corona. Commodore O'Hare wanted the zone closest the sun checked and Lieutenant Brett K. Johnson was going to take his scout close. Johnson was a mountain of a man squeezed in the left seat piloting the shuttle, his co-pilot, C.D., monitoring the instruments and sensors from the right seat. C.D. had told Brett what the C.D. stood for (it was, in fact, short for Chris Davis) a dozen times over the years they had worked together, but Brett couldn't seem to remember. He was every bit the pilot Brett was, but the smaller man was more attentive to the details on the sensors.

The glow of the sun shone through the filters over the cabin windows and reflected off Johnson's ever-present sunglasses. The prominences and flares were kind of pretty, he decided. If they weren't working, he might be tempted to try and fly under one. He had done that once, at a red star some years ago. It had scorched the ship pretty badly and disconcerted Command. They didn't court martial him or anything, but he and the rest of his crew had been transferred to rescue services.

C.D. and the Santino's were probably still pretty pissed off at him about that. But they'd never said anything, so Brett didn't worry.

C.D.'s station flashed a light and whistled. "Whoa, Brett, look at this," said his youthful-looking partner. Brett leaned over and gawked at C.D.'s screen

"Damn! What the heck is that?" Bret asked.

"I dunno," said C.D. "But it's big. Maybe the size of a command carrier." Over his shoulder he hollered: "Yo, Tino!"

"What?"

"Get up here, you gotta see this." C.D. yelled again.

"Can't," Santino answered. "Kid's on his sleep cycle and I got the watch."

"Wake Junior up, then get your ass up here, pronto," ordered Brett. "Need your eyeballs on this."

Ten minutes later, Santino climbed the ladder into the main cabin, grumbling. "Either of you hole-munchers ever hear of using the comm?"

"Got you up here, dint it?" answered C.D. "Check this out. What'd we find down here?"

The ship was massive, at least a mile long. The forward quarter was a tapered boom, with structure that appeared to be the bridge at the very end. Various boxes and probes jutted out of the boom. The aft three quarters was a colossal cylinder. Patches of plasma scoring dotted the sun-bleached hull. It seemed to be in disrepair; patches in the hull were evident, along with colored splotches. Three rectangular shuttle docks extended from the cylinder, the fourth was bent aft and buried in the hull. A star drive attached a third of the way up the exterior. The small engine pod made it clear the massive ship was grossly underpowered.

It wasn't dead. Here and there, windows glowed and flickered. "Let's take a look at the port side," instructed Santino. Johnson rotated the scout and arced over the ship. The glow of burning plasma erupted from a long slash where the port side nacelle had once been. The conflagration extended nearly to the stern. "Let's stay away from that fire," said C.D. Johnson agreed, pulling the scout up and over, inverted over the mystery ship.

"Boy!" yelled Santino. "Go in my stateroom, bring me the Jane's data pack."

The comm clicked. "I'm on watch, Pa," came a terse answer. "Go grab it yourself."

"Watch this," C.D. whispered to Brett as Santino flew out of his chair and dropped through the hatchway. C.D. switched on the comm to the lower deck. From the speakers came the sounds of slaps and punches, a low growl. "When I tell you to get me something, you drop what you're doing and frecking bring it to me!"

"Whattya know, the comm works," giggled Brett.

Santino returned to the bridge muttering under his breath about disobedient children and ungrateful bastards. The data stick in his console contained a record of all the ships registered in the Empire and a great many others registered with friends and foes alike. The small holo displayed showed ship after ship rapidly as

Santino shuffled through the record. He slowed the display, looking at the mystery ship and back at his holo. After forty minutes he grunted, pointing at the screen. "The *Xian*," he said. "About a hundred fifty years old. Started as a combat carrier, but the whole class was deemed a failure and sold off. *Xian* was converted to a gas collector and processor. He was pretty miserable at that, too, sold a half a dozen times before being retired by the Folsom Resources Company and sold for scrap five years ago."

"Yeah?" said Brett. "Then what the frack is it doing here?"

C.D. shrugged. "Orbiting," he suggested. "Unless a flare bursts in the next month, the *Xian's* orbit is pretty stable. Besides, with that plasma fire, he's as likely to blow up as not. Let's finish our sweep and head back to the fleet."

They all agreed and left the burning hulk behind. It would be a week before they reported the mysterious *Xian*.

Salvage began, along with recovery of the rescue pods. In each case, the process was similar. Scouts had mapped the debris field. Space jacks using work rigs grappled the wreckage. Mass calculations and material composition were checked and recorded. The wreckage was then pushed away on a trajectory toward other space jacks, who would maneuver the debris into massive rafts.

Cutters would follow after the larger pieces had been collected, pulling nets much like the fishermen of ancient Terra. When the nets were full enough, they were pulled out to the recycler ships where the materials were melted and compressed into blocks and attached to the tranches. Once the debris raft was large enough, a tug would be rigged and haul it to a salvage world to recycle the materials for the Empire.

Occasionally, a body collected in the net and a military shuttle summoned. A sniper would take aim from the shuttle airlock and put two rounds into the helmet. Then the body could be recovered and strapped to the hull for transport to *Respite*.

Commodore O'Hare was taking no chances. The three holed wrecks each had a frigate watching them. While she had troops available, she had sent a request for breeching units to clear the vessels of her unseen enemies before she sent her salvage crews in.

Doctor Ho-Bar scheduled a meeting with Katy aboard the *Tranquility*. They met in a medical theater, empty save for a sheet-covered body. "I thought you'd like to see what we're facing," he told her. "We've identified three species so far. This," he pulled the sheet back, "is clearly Terran. Sixty-five survivors, one hundred thirty-nine dead. Sixty-three of the survivors are Imperial Navy; we have them all in rehab tanks, and so interviewing them is out of the question for ten days. The other two survivors and all the dead are like this fellow."

The dead man had clearly been underfed, his skeletal rib cage indicated. His body was pocked with bruises and burns. Both arms were clearly broken, twisted at an awkward angle. "This one died of asphyxia," Ho-Bar reported. "He escaped his ship with a fully serviceable suit, but at some point, his oxygen was siphoned off. I'd guessing the broken arms were from fighting to keep his oxygen."

"Fighting who?" asked Katy. "Other Terrans?"

"Were it that simple." Ho-Bar led Katy to the next theater. A larger body lay on the table. He was at least seven feet tall and heavily muscled. Geometric shapes and tubes stretched and poked through his skin. There was a network of hoses or cables beneath the skin, connecting boxes and other odd shapes. Curiously, his head was a brilliant red and there were no features: no eyes, ears, nose or mouth. The other uncommon features were the two neat holes where the sniper had shot it in the head.

"What is…this?" asked the Commodore.

"What I believe we have here is a very advanced augmenton," the doctor said.

"An augmenton! First, Doctor, augmenton research was shut down more than a hundred years ago. The only ones found anywhere the Empire today are in laboratories or museums of atrocities. Certainly none of them are active or alive. They are extinct."

"Nevertheless, I have before you an augmenton who has expired in the last twenty-four hours. In the morgue I have another fifteen," declared Ho-Bar. "I also have fragments I believe come from several dozen more. The biologic components we recovered definitely have Terran DNA. I've preserved the mechanical components, including four living processors. I'll have them shipped to the Empire with the first raft."

"Very well," agreed Katy. "Send the biological components to recycling."

"Already being done."

"You said you had three aliens to show me," Katy said.

Ho-Bar looked at the floor and asked, "Katy, did you bring your flask with that swill?"

He took a long pull on the proffered flagon. "You're going to need a good stiff one for what's next."

Katy hesitated, took a drink. She followed the doctor through the ship to the shuttle bay. He looked her in the eye and asked, "Do you believe in monsters?"

She was taken aback. Before them was a covered cube, twenty feet to each side. "We had the wee people and fairies," she told him. "But then I grew up and stopped believing in such foolishness. My forty-year career hasn't dispelled that in the least. So whatever you have better be pretty scary."

Ho-Bar pulled at the cover. "You'll never look at your Aunt Matilda's cat the same, ever again," he said.

It was a large stasis cube. Katy gasped as the feline came into view. It hung suspended in the stasis field. Its head was easily a yard wide, its long, pointed ears laid flat. Its teeth were yellow, the fangs a foot long in a mouth frozen mid-scream. Long forelegs were spayed, as if it were reaching for Katy; five nine-inch scythe-like claws adorned each paw. The beast was at least nine feet long and looked poised mid-strike.

Clearly it was dead. Milky eyes followed Katy as she moved side to side, examining the cat. "Just what am I looking at here, Doctor?" she finally asked.

"One very big, very dead kitty," Ho-Bar responded. "We found it inside a rescue pod. We brought it onboard to study. It studied us for two days as we studied it. There were human remains in its digestive system. Apparently, not enough. It became agitated yesterday, clawing and throwing itself against the walls of the pod. Cracks began to form in the pod, so I made the decision to euthanize it. As you see, that decision agitated it even more before it succumbed.

"I ran a DNA scan. Curiously, it has a great deal of Terran in it. We'll do an autopsy, but I suspect it has a large brain. It's already demonstrated a degree of intelligence. Rescue pods don't launch themselves and it did bring sustenance to survive.

"Here's the bad news. Of the ten rescue pods outside, at least three have our super cats in them. Another one appears to have an augmenton. All of them have indications of Terrans, including the ones with the felines. I fear the worse for the Terrans, as we found in this one's pod, it appears they were brought along for lunch. We'll fill the pods with enough nozidrine gas to knock them out, then bring the pods aboard and examine them."

"I want the cats and augmentons dead," ordered Katy. "Imperial survivors send to *Respite* for recovery. Keep the alien Terrans here, confined. I'll send a detachment of soldiers to aid with security. Tan will come over and supervise the investigation. I want answers. These aren't Imperial citizens, so I want them confined."

"I'm not set up to be a prison, Commodore," stated the doctor.

"You're a medical facility, Doctor," Katy said. "You are better suited to aide Imperial Intelligence until we have the answers about the survivors."

"I will not permit torture."

"Agreed," Katy said. "But I want answers."

A soft chime sounded, followed by the tannoy. "Commodore O'Hare, you have a secure communication inbound. Priority Black Gamma."

Black Gamma. Intelligence, for certain, but Gamma?

"I have a secure suite, Katy," Ho-Bar said.

Katy locked the room and entered her security code. The holo twisted and a thick man appeared, dressed entirely in black. His head was broad and bald, and his resolved image revealed Imperial green Asiatic eyes. His brow thickened as the corners of his mouth forced themselves up into a rictus grin. "Commodore O'Hare! I am Intelligence Master Schwarz saKhan. I so look forward to meeting you. My convoy will arrive in half an hour. I have brought a breeching team and additional troops with me to aid in security while we investigate this nasty business. When I arrive, I want you and agent Tan aboard my ship immediately for a briefing."

"By whose authority, Master Schwarz?" queried Katy.

"One half hour, Commodore," came the terse response.

Chapter 9

A thin line of darkness appeared, opening through the fabric of space into otherspace. Fringed with indigo light, a dark, diamond-shaped ship passed through the space fold. The fold sealed without drama, leaving no trace. The black vessel, its surface was only marred by a miniscule symbol painted on its hull. The shield, superimposed over an image of Terra and a pair of crossed sabers, indicated an Imperial Intelligence ship glided alongside *Mary Kane*.

Katy admired the stealthy ship. It was a bit uncomfortable to the eye; the color was wrong, seemingly shifting from dark greys to black, to blacker still, then silvery grey again, nearly imperceptible. It had sleek lines, sliding alongside *Mary Kane* as a coiled beast of prey. Then it rotated suddenly, its docking tunnel extending into *Mary Kane*'s docking port.

Both vessels shuddered as they mated; on *Mary Kane*, the red warning light over the airlock shrieked. Atmosphere from both ships whooshed into the connection until green lights indicated the airlock was safe to open.

Tan placed her hand on the door switch. "Ready, Commodore?" she asked.

"Let's go," Katy said.

Tan touched the switch. *Mary Kane's* airlock opened with a noisy screech. A pair of black-clad soldiers greeted them, their helmets opaque, rifles aimed at the women's heads.

"Identification!" ordered one soldier. Tan handed a guard their identification cards. One at a time, the guard inserted the card into a data slot on his gauntlet. Satisfied for the moment, he waved them both into his black ship.

Thin white lines in the corners of the floor and ceiling provided enough illumination as they were led through the featureless interior. Another pair of guards stood at a portal where they were motioned inside.

Intelligence Master Schwartz saKhan lounged in a broad winged chair, a cut glass of amber liquid in his hand. A decanter and another glass sat on a low table before him, a second chair was to his right.

"Does she know who our enemies are?" Schwartz mind-spoke to Tan.

"No, Master. The physician has recovered some bodies of the Feloids, augmentons and slaves," Tan responded. **"Commodore O'Hare is resistant to my mental suggestion. However, she has ordered the execution of the augmentons and Feloids and recycling of the bodies. The slaves are being questioned in the main hospital."**

"You are personally to make sure the augmenton and Feloid remains are destroyed," he ordered. **"The Empire must not acquire that DNA. Understood?"**

"Yes, Master."

"Have any Sudahar been found yet?"

"No, Master."

"If any are found, I want them transferred here immediately."

"It shall be as you ordered, Master."

His face softened slightly. "It is good to see you again, Daughter."

"And you, Father."

"She has no knowledge of our relationship?"

"No, Father."

"Good. It works to our advantage at this point."

"Yes, Father."

The silent conversation took less than a second.

"Commodore O'Hare, welcome aboard *Loki*. I am, of course, Imperial Intelligence Master Schwartz sa-Khan." His grin appeared less forced then it had appeared on the comm. "Please, join me. May I offer you a drink?"

He poured a generous amount for Katy. "I call it the Demon's Crown. More than three millennia ago, some of my ancestors lived in what was called Saskatchewan along Duck Lake. A famous distiller there made a fine whiskey. Twice a year, my ancestors would purchase the casks used to age the whiskey, cut them in half and leach the whiskey from the oak. Years later, the distillery stopped selling the casks and processed the whiskey therein themselves, calling it the devil's cut. One advantage to being part of the Imperial Court: thirty years ago I purchased the property where the old distillery was and built a new one."

He took a sip of his drink and sighed happily. "The stock is quite exquisite and extraordinarily rare outside my own interests. If you like, I would be glad to give you a bottle, as a gift."

Katy took a cautious sip. Dear gods, exquisite wasn't the word! Having been drinking a poor version of a replicated Glivenich, this was offering iced sparkling to a being dying of thirst. The smoke was rich and neat, the bite delightful and the caramel tone was just enough to be noticed. She drank a bit more, wanting to quaff the whole glass at once. She mentally girded herself and took another tiny sip while trying not to eye the decanter.

"Marvelous, Intelligence Master," she said. "I shall look forward to your gift."

"Oh, Commodore, call me Schwartz, please!" he said. "I may call you Katy, yes? Good. Now, Katy, you are doubtlessly curious why the Intelligence Master would bother himself with such a mundane, yet important task of battlefield clean-up, yes?"

Katy settled back in the comfortable chair. "Indeed. I received little information on the combatants in this action, which is proving to be both a hindrance and a hazard to my task at hand. Can you provide me with any information as to whom I am dealing with, so I can send my salvage crews out with more confidence?"

"Certainly. Let me provide you with a little background information first." He tapped a console built into the arm of his chair; a holo star chart formed above them. "For the last two hundred fifty standard Imperial years, there have been numerous reports of thefts of starships in and along the Rim. This is not terribly uncommon; the region in question runs in and out of our borders. Outside, it is lawless region, few governments and fewer laws. The Empire is moving slowly into the Rim, gathering worlds into our sphere of influence and bringing peace and prosperity to those who accept us as their overlords.

"But the theft of a few ships wasn't considered extraordinary. At least, not until the last fifty years. I began to notice a pattern. A large number of otherspace-capable ships were stolen, mostly former warships. Many of them were recently retired, sent out for scrap, but stolen while they were still quite effective. I read the reports and supposed a clan of pirates were building muscle. But the ships weren't being seen after they were stolen.

"Ten years ago, a former fleet carrier turned refinery, the *Xian,* was stolen. The situation caught my attention. A ship of this sort can be used to supply a small fleet. I sent out more agents to investigate.

"We received reports of planets along the Rim being attacked. Mostly small colonies, barely worth noticing. But all the residents were either missing or dead. Commodities a

Battle Fleet might need were taken. But none of the attackers could be found, no trace of where they were hiding, no trace of who they were.

"Then we caught a major break. A message, in the open."

The recording of a clearly artificial voice said, *"This is Clementina. I am under attack at the third jump point. I can hold them off for a few days, but I will need your help escaping. Abandon the plan for now. Come to me, my children, I need your help."*

"Messages from the stolen ships gave us this point as a staging area. The Imperial Fleet had an entire battlegroup waiting. This was no battle, it was a massacre. Thirty-five stolen ships were destroyed here. However a few ships escaped, including *Xian*.

"We lost a cruiser and a pair of frigates.

"I will provide you with the transponder signals from the Imperial ships so you'll be able to distinguish our rescue pods from theirs. The rest are enemy and are to be destroyed."

"We have survivors," Katy reported. "Terran, it seems…"

"They are not Terrans," Schwartz ordered. "They are the enemy. They are to be killed."

"There are other species as well," said Katy. "Augmentons, giant cats."

"The augmentons were declared an abomination a thousand years ago," said Schwartz. "As such, they are to be destroyed on sight. Your giant cats are known as Feloids. They are a genetic construct from beyond the Rim. I have sufficient information on them and they are to be destroyed on sight. I have also sufficient information on the humanoids. They are not Terran. I have declared them an alien threat to the Empire. You will kill them and have their bodies recycled. Immediately. Do I make myself clear, Commodore?"

Katy stood. "I am bound by the Laws of Angkor Khan with regard to the treatment of prisoners," she said stiffly. "Further, I am a naval officer and I am bound by both regulations and the laws of the space traveler. I will execute the augmentons and the cats as you wish. I will not summarily execute Terrans without a formal review."

"You are a disgraced *former* naval officer who my cousin, the Khan, has a curious infatuation for. I am a scion of the Imperial line. I have held the review and found them guilty of being non-Terran captives," Schwartz dictated. "As a member of the court and of Imperial rank, I have condemned them to death. I have a troopship with breeching pods arriving within the hour, Commodore. They will clear the three remaining enemy ships of any potential enemy and they will patrol local space, hunting down any surviving combatants. You are to continue your salvage operation and support my troops in any way they may require. Do you understand?"

"Yes, Sir."

"Then you are dismissed."

Katy turned, stopping when Schwartz called, "Oh, Commodore." A black uniformed soldier appeared before her, handing her a purple velvet bag. It gurgled enticingly.

"Don't forget your gift," Schwartz told her.

Brett Johnson swung the scout with élan around the trussed equipment sled towed by the *Mary Kane.* All the tugs in Katy's recovery fleet towed the sleds. The amount of gear needed to perform a decent salvage operation was staggering, from miles of carbon composite cable to boost motor packs for moving larger pieces of debris. Had the equipment been carried internally, at least three dozen more tugs would have been required.

The towed sled also provided docking points for scouts, cutters and shuttles along with transit tubes so the smaller ships' crews could visit the considerably larger tugs. Johnson, C.D. and the Santino's swam through the zero-g passage to the *Mary Kane.*

C.D. turned the scout's report file to *Mary Kane's* resource officer and wandered below to find the rest of his crew in the wardroom shoveling down lunch. The elder Santino had stopped by Engineering, and a small bottle of hooch brewed by the *Mary Kane's* engineers sat in the middle of the table. C.D. poured himself a glass as a porter set his lunch on the table.

The non-regulation moonshine was rocket fuel with a nuclear fire aftertaste. On a regular naval vessel, brew like this would get the still operator thrown into the brig. In the salvage fleet, every ship had at least one still and was not shy about competing with sister ships for the title of best hooch. The *Mary Kane's* engineers were proud of their popular concoction.

While they ate, the analysts went through the scout's report. A gasp swept through the chamber as the holo image of the *Xian* appeared. The image spun and swirled, reflecting Johnson's manipulation of his scout around the burning hulk. First Officer Bosley was summoned, who in turn contacted Katy. They ran the record through for her once before she bolted for the wardroom carrying a portable holo emitter.

"Why in god's name didn't you report this immediately?" demanded Katy, flicking on the emitter. *Xian* burned above the bottle of hooch.

"Ma'am, our mission was to investigate the inner region along the photosphere for survivors and derelicts," said Johnson. "There were intermittent power indications, but no signals or obvious signs of life."

"The ship is venting hydrogen and has a severe plasma fire in the area of the compound reactors," said C.D.

"The port side engine is missing. Given the plasma fire, I'm pretty sure the ship has either exploded or broken into pieces and fallen into the sun

Both Santino's nodded vigorously.

Katy closed her eyes and exhaled, loud in the sudden silence. "If your lunch is finished," she said, "get back to your ship and go run me a full survey on *Xian*. Understood, Lieutenant?"

"Just finishing now, Ma'am." The whole scout crew stood and slid towards the door.

"Lieutenant?"

"Yes, Ma'am?"

Katy pointed, "Is there something wrong with your hooch?"

"No, Ma'am."

"It would be a great insult to *Mary Kane* if you left it behind." Katy said, the corners of her mouth upturned. "I might even take it as a personal insult."

"Yes, Ma'am." Johnson grabbed the bottle and fled out the door.

The holo of the burning *Xian* wobbled and settled back, hovering over the table.

"Jhon?" Katy called over the comm.

"Commodore?"

"Call a holo council of all the tug captains and salvage engineers in seventy-two hours."

hooch brewed by the *Mary Kane's* engineers sat in the middle of the table. C.D. poured himself a glass as a porter set his lunch on the table.

The non-regulation moonshine was rocket fuel with a nuclear fire aftertaste. On a regular naval vessel, brew like this would get the still operator thrown into the brig. In the salvage fleet, every ship had at least one still and was not shy about competing with sister ships for the title of best hooch. The *Mary Kane's* engineers were proud of their popular concoction.

While they ate, the analysts went through the scout's report. A gasp swept through the chamber as the holo image of the *Xian* appeared. The image spun and swirled, reflecting Johnson's manipulation of his scout around the burning hulk. First Officer Bosley was summoned, who in turn contacted Katy. They ran the record through for her once before she bolted for the wardroom carrying a portable holo emitter.

"Why in god's name didn't you report this immediately?" demanded Katy, flicking on the emitter. *Xian* burned above the bottle of hooch.

"Ma'am, our mission was to investigate the inner region along the photosphere for survivors and derelicts," said Johnson. "There were intermittent power indications, but no signals or obvious signs of life."

"The ship is venting hydrogen and has a severe plasma fire in the area of the compound reactors," said C.D.

"The port side engine is missing. Given the plasma fire, I'm pretty sure the ship has either exploded or broken into pieces and fallen into the sun

Both Santino's nodded vigorously.

Katy closed her eyes and exhaled, loud in the sudden silence. "If your lunch is finished," she said, "get back to your ship and go run me a full survey on *Xian*. Understood, Lieutenant?"

"Just finishing now, Ma'am." The whole scout crew stood and slid towards the door.

"Lieutenant?"

"Yes, Ma'am?"

Katy pointed, "Is there something wrong with your hooch?"

"No, Ma'am."

"It would be a great insult to *Mary Kane* if you left it behind." Katy said, the corners of her mouth upturned. "I might even take it as a personal insult."

"Yes, Ma'am." Johnson grabbed the bottle and fled out the door.

The holo of the burning *Xian* wobbled and settled back, hovering over the table.

"Jhon?" Katy called over the comm.

"Commodore?"

"Call a holo council of all the tug captains and salvage engineers in seventy-two hours."

Chapter 10

The strongback of any tug vessel, from ancient times when workhorse boats plied the oceans of Terra to modern Imperial tugs like the *Mary Kane,* all had one common feature. The most critical point of the tug was the connection of the object being towed and the small, powerful ship.

Mary Kane's engineering deck served as the nexus for him and his four brother ships in Katy's fleet. The space was the largest on the ship, an uneven hexagon, four one hundred-yard walls with twenty-five-yard walls angled at each corner. The room was also a hundred yards deep, with four heavy star drive pylons mounted at the center of each long wall.

Its designers had carefully considered the heavy work that was to be done in engineering, so they subtly installed and adjusted the gravity plates on each bulkhead. There was no up or down in this chamber, no floor or ceiling. Every bulkhead was a gravitational plane. An object could not fall from one end of the room to the other; seven other gravity planes would exert sufficient pull to arrest the fall of personnel or equipment. Any heavy equipment was easily moved from on section to the other, balanced on eight gravity fields. Inertia had to be considered, of course. A one-ton towing stay had the inertia of a one ton towing stay no matter which direction it was being moved. Hence, heavy equipment was moved carefully. Additionally, the computers controlling the gravity plates monitored any falling object and would compensate to prevent damage or injury.

The feature was new to Imperial tugs. It was not only an efficient use of space but, once mastered, the multiple planes of gravity made for great sport, leaping and twisting in the shifting gravity. There was never a shortage of volunteers to serve on Imperial heavy tugs.

Non-engineers and new crewmen often developed vertigo until they learned how to maneuver the odd gravity or avoided engineering entirely.

Because it was the largest open space on *Mary Kane*, engineering was used for meetings and briefings. Today, the nine other Captains and their engineers and tow masters joined Katy, Johan and *Mary Kane's* Chief Engineer, Danny Diezac. Engineer Diezac was a slight man with boyish looks and a northern Occident accent. Widely admired throughout the fleet for his engineering prowess, he had a quiet confidence and easy demeanor.

Engineer Diezac had been Katy's first choice when she took over the *Mary Kane*. One look around his sanctum was enough to see why. For all the dirty work one would presume to happen on a tug, Danny Diezac demanded his engineering be kept spotless. Pale white walls were adorned with every placard centered exactly where it was supposed to be. The manual tow bollards were painted, each position bearing the time honored maritime tradition for their position: red to port, green to starboard. Every piece of equipment was labeled and secured. Work stations and benches with handy tools were spread across the deck.

Three sixty-foot holograms of the *Xian* floated in the center of the room. The captains, engineers and tow masters of all ten tugs assembled comfortably around the images, a glass of *Mary Kane's* hooch in the hand, paw or claw of each officer who could tolerate alcohol. For those who couldn't, such as the crab-like Henerite, captain of the medium tug *Taiho,* various inebriants had been provided. Having worked with Commodore O'Hare for many years, each officer knew these types of meetings would be both serious and social affairs. They were to enjoy themselves, foster friendships and build team working skills. But if an officer should become too drunk, the Commodore was infamous for dropping the offender off at the first world the fleet came across.

Whether it had an atmosphere or not.

Intelligence Master Swartz and *Mary Kane's* Intelligence officer Tan were also present, though Swartz looked uncomfortable in the shifting gravity planes of the room. He had found a work station and seated himself, looking fairly green and miserable as the beings around him jumped and flipped from floor to ceiling to wall with practiced ease.

Katy pursed her lips and whistled. "All right, let's get this briefing started," she ordered. "Here he is, the former Imperial Mega Heavy Carrier *Xian,* former tanker, former refiner, former scrapheap…you get the idea. Now he's in close orbit to Joeanmika 46, a Wolfe star, after a battle with other stolen ships. The why of how he came here isn't any of our concern. How to get her up to an orbit where we can either prepare her for tow or scrap her in place is the discussion. Dan?"

Engineer Diezac stepped forward. Pointing at the three images, he said, "Here's the progression of *Xian* as best we can tell. First is when *Xian* first came out of the yards, a spanking new man-o-war. He sure was pretty, but poorly designed and grossly underpowered. Even after adding a pair of breeder reactors, he still suffered from rolling power outages. After three engagements where four of her sister ships were destroyed, the class was pulled from service and converted to tankers.

"They were even more miserable in that role, so one hundred years ago, the remaining three of the class were sold. Two were scrapped outright; the *Xian* was converted into a gas refinery ship as you see in this second model. Banks of conversion reactors, fifty in all, were installed in his primary hull along with two hundred storage tanks for the various gases he was to mine from gas planets. Clearly, he was unsuited for this role, too; he was sold a half-dozen times before he was finally dumped at a scrap yard in the Rim sixteen years ago.

"Ten years ago, *Xian* was reported stolen. Though why anyone would want to steal this piece of gungar shyte is beyond me."

The whole room reverberated with laughter.

"Here is how he appears today." Diezac pressed a stud on his pad and the two newer versions of *Xian* melted away. The first image swelled to one hundred eighty feet. "Three scouts are orbiting her right now, sending us this image. You can see the damage, both from the poor upkeep over the years and the damage from the battle. Further, he's been taking a pretty heavy dose of various radiations from the Wolfe star for several weeks, so there's no saying exactly what condition his structure is in. Gyona?"

A Mykonos trotted up to Dan. "I am Gyona Philemon, Tow Master of the *Taiho,*" she said. "I have studied the information provided about the *Xian* and have come up with a salvage plan."

"Why are you using that dog?" called Intelligence Master Swartz.

The room went silent. Katy's eyes bored in Swartz's direction. "Gyona has been in my service thirteen years," she declared. "Before that, she was a brilliant engineer in the Fleet for twenty years until a fire on her ship crippled her lungs. She taught at the Imperial Engineering College for ten years before signing on with us.

"Further, Gyona has earned both the respect and friendship of every being in this room. And, as I recall, Mykonos Three has been a member of the Empire for nearly four hundred years. Is that good enough for you, Spy Master?"

Swartz took a sip of his drink. "Do carry on," he ordered.

Gyona bared her teeth momentarily, then continued. "We're hampered by three big problems. The first is the fire in the conversion reactors. We can't operate within one hundred yards of them for now. When we get *Xian* to a safer orbit, we can send a team in and start ejecting them.

"Problem two: The Wolfe star is in remission, but still is ejecting radiations at levels far too high for space jacks to work safely in. I have taken the liberty to order a half mile square mylomicron blanket which will provide limited protection. Still, each space jack will be limited to one-hour shifts, then require a day on *Tranquility* for recovery. We'll need to move *Tranquility* closer to the operation.

"The third issue is *Xian* herself. I can assume a great deal about her physical condition from our scans, but without being able enter the ship and do a physical survey, we run the risk of *Xian* breaking up as we lift her to a higher orbit.

"So we are going to do this gently. We'll erect the radiation shield as soon as it arrives. The first debris raft is ready, so after *Lisalui* rigs it, he'll transfer his space jacks around the fleet tugs, so we have their manpower. *Lydia Rae* and *Daisy Mae* will mount fifty propulsion packs to the starboard side of the aft hull and hardwire them to the forward hull. *Kinterkae* will mount twenty-five propulsion packs to the port side of the forward hull. *China Girl* will assemble the rig for the actual tow. He'll be joined by *Lydia Rae* in the pull position. *Luna Sea* and *Tatoosh* will rig to the forward hull.

"When we're set, we'll use the propulsion packs with *Luna Sea* and *Tatoosh* to turn *Xian* to starboard. As he comes about to our desired tow angle, about 1.6 degrees off her current orbit, *Lydia Rae* and *Daisy Mae* will start the pull, assisted by *Luna Sea* and *Tatoosh* as *Xian* comes to bear. We'll use the tugs for the main pull and the propulsion packs to slow him once he reaches our desired orbit."

The holo of *Xian* followed Gyona's narrative, disappearing out of the starboard side of engineering, pulled by four tiny tugs.

"We'll pull him out to the orbit near the fourth planet," said Katy. "We'll park him there and resume the rest of the salvage. The Army will board *Xian* and check for alien survivors. Once it's clear, we'll board a team, led by Engineers Diezac and Gyona, to make up the salvage plan. Questions?"

"Seventy-five p-packs are nearly all of our stock," said Captain Verdiane of the *China Girl.* "What's that going to do for the rest of the salvage? We're going to need those packs for the other debris rafts we're building now."

"*Lisalui* will mate up with a new sled before he returns in four weeks' time," confirmed Katy. "I've already sent out the call to the sector Governors asking for every available propulsion pack they can get their hands on. I've even asked a few back-door assets I know. We'll know in four weeks what we have to work with."

"What about the troops? That is a lot of ship to inspect before we can get to work." The question came from the engineer of the *Jitterbug,* one of the new medium tugs assigned to Katy's fleet.

"We have one boarding ship available now, with two breeching pods," Intelligence Master Swartz said. "I've contacted the sector Imperial Army Corps. Two more troop transports with two more boarding ships are enroute."

"That's an awful lot of troops, Master Swartz," said Katy.

"As your officer pointed out, the *Xian* is an awful lot of ship," he replied.

The salvage fleets officers looked at each other with apprehension. Never had they ever seen anyone speak to the Commodore in that fashion. Not without someone being unceremoniously knocked on their ass. Or dumped on the nearest rock floating by.

The holo of the *Xian* appeared again, nearly filling the space. "Let's keep in mind the mission," said Jhon Bosley. "Get the *Xian* into a safe orbit, then resume the rest of the salvage. Let's focus on that and worry about the rest later." With that, the officers moved around the hologram and examined it closely.

The tension broken, Katy leaped, twisted and landed in front of Swartz. "Why all the troops, Spy Master?" she asked.

"Why the mechanical rigs to tow the ship?" asked Swartz instead of answering. "The Imperial fleet ships use tractor beams to haul cripples from a battle zone."

"A cruiser is grossly overpowered," Katy explained. "A tractor beam requires incredible amounts of power. A warship can expend this energy to tow a cripple to a safe area, then leave it for a salvage fleet. Not even a command carrier has enough energy to pull a ship the size of a destroyer to a salvage yard. Our methods are the ones used since ancient times, tried and proven. This ship," she waved her arm around, "is the pinnacle of those methods. The equipment you see around you can be configured for specific loads and missions. *Mary Kane* and her sisters each have four star drives comparable to the ones used on the latest dreadnaughts. Our medium tugs have three-star drives. By comparison, any one of these ships carry more raw power than the power plants onboard the *Xian*. If we are going to haul a wreck from perilous orbit, we're going to use proven methods and equipment. Satisfied?"

Swartz sipped his drink and nodded. "Very good, Commodore." He made his way to his feet, leaning heavily on the workstation.

"You didn't answer my officer's question," Katy said. "Why so many troops?"

"I am using ancient and proven methods and equipment, Commodore." He tapped two fingers to his forehead and wobbled from workstation to workstation to the exit portal.

Chapter 11

Breathe in. Pain.

Breathe out. Agony.

Oh God, please, let me hold my breath. I can't stand the pain.

But the spike forces me. I can't hold my breath, I won't stop breathing.

Breathe in. Pain.

Air racing in through my nostrils and mouth. Fire down my windpipe. Pooling acid in my lungs. The pain, oh God, the pain!

Breathe out. Agony.

The acid rises, fills my mouth and sinus with fresh, searing fire.

My body is an exposed, raw nerve of throbbing pain. The straps they hung about my chest and shoulders crush me. I'm certain my skin must be rubbed raw by now, the weight of my body hanging from the accursed straps. How anything else could hurt more, I couldn't imagine. But I didn't need to imagine.

Breathe in. Pain.

Breathe out. Agony.

The spike in the back of my neck. The voices had said it wouldn't hurt, that I would lose consciousness as the micro cilia worked through my brain. The micro cilia certainly worked its way through my brain. Only instead of rendering me unconscious, the cilia worked at finding each nerve ending which would send torment throughout my body.

Each and every nerve ending.

I am most certainly conscious of every moment. Worse still, I'm not allowed to sleep. The spike ensures that. When I feel myself starting to escape into the blissful freedom of unconsciousness, the spike stimulates a nerve cluster and I am shocked back into wakefulness.

I can't even scream. I have no control. I can feel every fiber of my body, I can see everything in my field of vision, hear every noise around me.

Breathe in. Pain.

Breathe out. Agony.

In that field of vision, I see one man directly across from me, naked, save for the harness suspending him inches above the deck. His spike holds his head up, blank eyes stare into mine. I can see whole or parts of five men to either side of him. They all have a port just below their breastbone like I do. They all have shunts in each arm, as have I.

Out of the corners of my eyes, I can see a man to each side. I can't focus or move my eyes, so I can only assume they are naked, hung and spiked, too.

I divide my "day" into three segments. The men in the blue shorts move down the passage with a hose. I have no control of my bowels, so they spray the urine and feces off my legs. A pair of the men come by later with a wagon carrying a tank with a hose. They *connect it to the port below my breast bone and "feed" me. The pain of hunger is then replaced by the agony of my stomach being force fed and the torture of my digestive tract processing my "meal" and expelling it.*

The third event is always the most painful if that were possible. Doctor Dander Palm has survived. He draws blood from one stint in my arm and places it in a device he carries. He studies it, then inserts a needle in the shunt, forcing in still more acid.

He speaks to me in low tones. At first, I could hardly understand him through his tears. As time passed, he became less emotional. "I know you can't hear me, Lars," he would say. "I should stop talking to you. It's not good for either one of us. But maybe there's a spark of you in there. I'm sorry, so very sorry. I shouldn't have left you and your family. It wouldn't have made too much a difference. I'd be hanging there with you, I guess, instead of being a slave to the Sudahar."

A horrible day. "I saw your daughters today, Lars," he said. "I wish I hadn't. They're alive, after a fashion. It's horrible, just horrible. I'm sorry, Lars, I know you'd want me to kill them if you saw what they're doing to them. But I can't, they won't let me get close enough. But I will, I promise you, if I can get a chance."

The day I discovered why we were here. A Feloid, that's what the giant cats are called, came stalking by. He sniffed me and moved on. Minutes later I heard a heavy noise, like a sack of grain dropped on the barn floor. The Feloid stalked through my vision again. One of our number, the wires of his spike dangling from the back of his head as the Feloid dragged it past me. It had already pulled off the poor man's arm and was chewing on it.

Feed. We were in storage to feed them on their journey. The spike in our heads, the hanging us on the wall; all to keep us compliant and controlled until a Feloid gets hungry.

The day of the battle. I was agonizing as the slaves hosed me down. Surely, I should be mad by now! Between the lack of sleep and the torturous, continuous agony, surely, I must have gone mad. But even insanity was being denied me.

An alarm sounded. The lights flashed and dimmed. The slaves dropped their hoses and ran. The ship shook and rattled, we all swung wildly, I struck the men to my left and right. My mind screamed as the pain increased, if it were possible.

Agony! Agony! Agony! Horrid noises, the ship would shudder, then we would be swinging again.

I was not fed. No doctor appeared to pump poisons into me. Hunger manifested itself as a new, different pain. I could acutely feel thirst. My mind screamed as I hoped I was dying at last.

The ship stopped shaking. The lights flickered, bathing us in bursts of hellish bright light, then plunging us in to blackness. The battery powered emergency lights had died long ago. It was quiet. Far off noises reverberated, but I didn't know what they were.

Doctor Palm and the slaves returned. "They're gone, Lars," he said. "The Empire was lying in wait. The fleet has been destroyed. The Feloids and their red heads are gone. None of us know how to drive the ship. We're falling into the sun. We'll all be dead soon, Lars. You, me, your daughters, everyone. I'm sorry, Lars."

He fell to his knees, crying.
He's sorry.
If I could, I would spit on him.
Breathe in. Pain!
Breathe out. Agony!

Tan had attached herself to the Mykonos engineer, Gyona, at Master Swartz's suggestion. Gyona didn't mind and found herself teaching the young Terran agent while supervising the salvage of *Xian*. Tan was full of questions that the elderly engineer calmly answered, instructing as she had at the academy before employment with Commodore O'Hare.

The mylomicron blanket arrived. Tan watched wide-eyed as the bundle was positioned between the sun and the *Xian*. Gyona checked her displays and ordered, "O.K. Deploy."

The bundle unfolded, then unfolded again and again. It continued to wiggle and flop as it grew larger and larger until it was its full half mile square. "Position good from here," a space jack reported. "Centered nicely on the target, don't see any rips or tears."

"O.K. nice job, Willie," Gyona commended. "Best you and your crew jet over to *Respite* and take your swim in the regen gel."

"Gotchya, Gyona," came the reply. "See you tomorrow."

The tugs and the space jacks swarmed *Xian,* appearing as toys along her sides. Gyona oversaw the work from *Jitterbug's* engineering. The installation of the propulsion packs was going quicker than estimated. "Normally, we would bolt the packs from the inside and out," she explained to Tan. "Since we don't have access to the interior, we're burning the paint away and bonding the packs into place with a molecular adhesive. We can get the packs installed quicker, but the security will be in question. We'll likely lose some of the propulsion packs."

She focused on a group of space jacks maneuvering a pack into position, a white dome, twenty feet around with a flat cylinder atop it. "Normally we would operate them remotely when we're using them on a hulk or a raft," Gyona lectured, "but with all the hard radiation, I'm afraid the signals might get corrupted. So we'll lay hardlines forward to the tow line and operate the packs aboard *Taiho.*"

"Will the angle you're turning the ship be enough, Engineer?" asked Tan. "1.8 degrees doesn't seem anywhere near enough to achieve a safe orbit."

The Mikoyan engineer's eyes twinkled, and a noise of amusement issued from her throat. "You don't study orbital mechanics at your Intelligence school, do you?" she asked. "How about physics or the basic laws of gravity? No matter. Let's see…"

Gyona leaped to a work bench, dug about and bounded back to Tan with a spool of wire and a large wrench. She tied the wrench to a length of wire. "Step back, would you?" The Mykosian swung the wrench in a small circle. "This is *Xian* and I am the sun," she said. "The ship is moving pretty quick, but my photosphere is exerting drag on my wrench, slowing it." She spun the wrench slower. "What will happen next?"

"Easy," Tan said. "The wrench falls into the sun."

"Exactly. So what I need to do is speed up the wrench to keep it from hitting me, yes?" Gyona began to spin the wrench faster. "Now what happens?"

"The wrench stays in orbit around you."

"Indeed, but eventually, my arm gets tired and friction develops again," the engineer said. "Right back where we started. What does the wrench want to do?"

"It wants to swing wider," Tan said. "Increase the orbit. So why don't you have the tugs just pull it at a sharper angle away from the sun?"

"A fair question," Gyona said as she let the wrench slow itself. "What is the condition inside *Xian*?"

"I don't know."

"I don't know, either," said Gyona. "So we alter the angle enough, so we can increase the speed of *Xian* and let her pull the string out, so to speak. It's a matter of orbital physics and energy conservation. As my old grandfather used to say, why work any harder than you need to?"

As she mentioned her grandfather, Tan noticed Gyona touched her odd hat. "If I may ask, why do you wear that cap?"

The Mikoyan looked pensive. "History tells us Mikonos was not always a member, or even a friend of the great Terran Empire," she said. "Outsiders from the Galactic Council came to our world and convinced our council to arm and defy Terra. Philemon disagreed and spoke against making war with Terra. When the regents fleet came to Mykonos, we were being slaughtered, although the weapons the outsiders gave us were doing great damage to the Imperial fleet. On the fourth day, when all seemed lost, the Crown Princess herself contacted our government with an offer of peace. Fortunately for us, Philemon was the sole survivor of our council and readily agreed to the peace. Later, Philemon journeyed to Terra for the coronation of the Crown Princess to Queen. He saw the marvels of the Empire and became determined to elevate Mykonos beyond that of a client state. He wanted us to stand proudly as equals in the Empire.

"He spent his life, cajoling and convincing our people to move to the future. After the Empire helped us rebuild our society, he sent the best and the brightest to the Empire to learn. Those learned returned and taught those who would become our teachers. We built schools, then universities and laboratories. One hundred years after the Empire sought to destroy us, we earned our invitation to join them.

Philemon the Great didn't live to see Mykonos join the Empire. He was already old when he saw the Queen crowned.

Gyona leaped to a work bench, dug about and bounded back to Tan with a spool of wire and a large wrench. She tied the wrench to a length of wire. "Step back, would you?" The Mykosian swung the wrench in a small circle. "This is *Xian* and I am the sun," she said. "The ship is moving pretty quick, but my photosphere is exerting drag on my wrench, slowing it." She spun the wrench slower. "What will happen next?"

"Easy," Tan said. "The wrench falls into the sun."

"Exactly. So what I need to do is speed up the wrench to keep it from hitting me, yes?" Gyona began to spin the wrench faster. "Now what happens?"

"The wrench stays in orbit around you."

"Indeed, but eventually, my arm gets tired and friction develops again," the engineer said. "Right back where we started. What does the wrench want to do?"

"It wants to swing wider," Tan said. "Increase the orbit. So why don't you have the tugs just pull it at a sharper angle away from the sun?"

"A fair question," Gyona said as she let the wrench slow itself. "What is the condition inside *Xian*?"

"I don't know."

"I don't know, either," said Gyona. "So we alter the angle enough, so we can increase the speed of *Xian* and let her pull the string out, so to speak. It's a matter of orbital physics and energy conservation. As my old grandfather used to say, why work any harder than you need to?"

As she mentioned her grandfather, Tan noticed Gyona touched her odd hat. "If I may ask, why do you wear that cap?"

The Mikoyan looked pensive. "History tells us Mikonos was not always a member, or even a friend of the great Terran Empire," she said. "Outsiders from the Galactic Council came to our world and convinced our council to arm and defy Terra. Philemon disagreed and spoke against making war with Terra. When the regents fleet came to Mykonos, we were being slaughtered, although the weapons the outsiders gave us were doing great damage to the Imperial fleet. On the fourth day, when all seemed lost, the Crown Princess herself contacted our government with an offer of peace. Fortunately for us, Philemon was the sole survivor of our council and readily agreed to the peace. Later, Philemon journeyed to Terra for the coronation of the Crown Princess to Queen. He saw the marvels of the Empire and became determined to elevate Mykonos beyond that of a client state. He wanted us to stand proudly as equals in the Empire.

"He spent his life, cajoling and convincing our people to move to the future. After the Empire helped us rebuild our society, he sent the best and the brightest to the Empire to learn. Those learned returned and taught those who would become our teachers. We built schools, then universities and laboratories. One hundred years after the Empire sought to destroy us, we earned our invitation to join them.

Philemon the Great didn't live to see Mykonos join the Empire. He was already old when he saw the Queen crowned.

Shortly after he returned, he went into the forest to die, as is our way. When we graduate his university, we take his name as our own and don the cap of Philemon for our people."

They sat quietly for nearly an hour, monitoring the progress. Finally, Gyona said, "I am over ninety standard years old now, older than Philemon the Great was when he walked into the forest. When this mission is complete, I shall return home to Mykonos. My time to take the walk has come."

After ten standard days, Gyona announced the work was finished. "I have only to perform a last inspection, then we will be ready to lift *Xian* to a stable orbit."

Jitterbug moved close to *Xian as* Gyona and Tan donned their spacesuits. Gyona's was old, made specifically for a Mykosian, and adorned with dozens of patches of other missions and ships she'd been assigned. Tan's was a standard Terran issue. Down the *Jitterbug's* gravity-less equipment boom to the airlock they swam, where mounted to the boom were dozens of space jack frames.

A space jack frame was the standard extra vehicular vessel used by the Empire. The operator climbed inside the open globe frame, clips securing the frame to the spacesuit. Behind the operator was the power supply. The globe rotated on all three axis, so the need to turn the vessel wasn't necessary. Four articulated arms extended at right angles to each other, each ending with a five fingered "hand" for gripping and manipulating tools and equipment.

While *Jitterbug* was a fairly new ship, his well-worn rigs and bright yellow paint were chipped and scraped. Repairs had been done to the rigs and left unpainted. Gyona and Tan each selected a charged rig, fastened herself in and sallied to *Xian*.

As they moved closer to the gigantic hull of the ship, Tan became apprehensive. She thought she could hear the buzzing of a small insect in her helmet. She craned her head about, searching for the tiny bug. She stopped, feeling foolish, reminding herself insects couldn't fly in zero g. Still, she was certain she could hear something.

They examined the harness where the *Lydia Rae* and *China Girl* would be joined to *Xian*. The wrappings satisfied the engineer; they jetted over to the harness for *Luna Sea* and *Tatoosh*. Gyona sent a thumb up with her space jack arm to the working space jacks, pleased with their work.

Now they progressed toward the stern to examine the propulsion pack field on the starboard side. They flew quickly, as their hour time limit was drawing to a close.

Tan's uneasy feeling intensified. The buzzing had been replaced with a low, dull throb pounding in her head. Not like a headache, more of a noise in her head she couldn't quite hear. The further aft they traveled, the more unsettled she became and the more aware of the throb she couldn't hear.

They were nearly to the main hull when the throb turned into a terrified scream. A pair of screams in pain. An agonizing dozen screams. A hundred screams tormented by an unseen horror. Tan's jack rig crashed into the hull as the cacophony multiplied again.

"Agent Tan are you all right?" Gyona asked.

Tan fell out of her jack rig and began to crawl across *Xian's* hull. Thousands of screams filled her head. She fell to her side and curled in a ball, her scream joining the choir of the Damned that only she could hear.

Chapter 12

She ran down the dark corridor screaming.

Lights flashed intermittently as she bounced off uneven walls in her panicked flight. The Damned were all around her, moaning, crying and weeping. Hands grabbed at her from the walls and the floor.

Tan ran full speed and face first into a wall, dropping her to the floor stunned. Bracing against the wall, she staggered to her feet and found the walls had closed her in. "No," she cried, pounding at them. The demons mocked her and began calling her name in mindspeak.

"**Tan! TAN!**"

She slid down the wall beaten, bawling, face buried in her hands. They knew her! The torment would never end now. "Stop!" she wailed, "Stop!"

"**Tan!**" The demon called again. "**Tan! Sister! Stop this foolishness this instant. Father and your Commodore are very cross. You will wake up now, this instant. Open your eyes, now!**"

"No…"

"**NOW, Tan!**" repeated the demon.

Claws gripped her eyelids and tore them open. Tan gasped; the demon had her own face! "**T… Tuhnka?**" Her mind gasped.

"Of course, you foolish girl," her face smirked. **"I was in the sector, so Father summoned me to wake you. He has forbidden me from killing you in this condition. So wake now and get out of this bed. Your Commodore and our father want answers.**

When you are recovered, Father has said I can remove you from the competition. After I have killed you, there will only be five of us left!"

The screams faded. Tan willed herself to sit up. Her sister touched the comm and announced, "She is awake."

Doctor Ho-Bar, Commodore O'Hare and Intelligence Master Swartz…Father, surrounded her bed. The doctor waved an instrument over her, nodding his approval. "As I suspected," he rumbled. "She suffered a severe psychosomatic event. No physical damage, but I suspect she'll need some time to regain her mental equilibrium."

"No." said Swartz saKhan. "She has been conditioned for this type of event. Agent Tan, go clean yourself, don your uniform and make your report, immediately."

"Yes, Master." Tan staggered out of the bed to the bathroom. She stripped swiftly and entered the shower. A soft chime sounded, followed by a comforting voice, "Doctor Ho-Bar has ordered a ten-minute therapeutic shower. It begins now." A soft, warm waterfall cascaded down from the ceiling. Tan arched her back, the shower of warmth poured over her face and through her hair. A stream washed over her breasts and along her stomach, tumbling over her slender hips and down her legs.

The gentle cascade turned to a pulsing torrent, tapping her flesh in a slow rhythm that picked up pace. And began shooting from the walls as well. Tan placed her hands on the wall in front of her and arched her back as a cat would stretch. The torrent continued, pounding her tired, sore muscles.

She began to reflect on the events while she was being chased by the Damned. The memory was there, sheathed by her natural defenses, a thin veneer of a shield protecting her from the madness and pain within. She touched it lightly, like probing a broken tooth with her tongue. The pain was staggering, she was fortunate to be leaning on the wall. Immediately she placed another thicker, stronger shield in place. Tan looked inwardly at the memory, deciding what she should do. Clearly, for her own protection, she should place so many shields over it that not even a Mind Master would be able to break it.

Her father's words came to her. *"Of what use is this? Can it be put to good use? Is it something you could use as a weapon?"*

A weapon, yes. She removed the new shields, back to the original, natural and barely effect protection. She reconstructed a new shield over it, plain and prosaic to any who would try and read it. She layered in a lie sure to attract Tuhnka and perhaps father as well, should he look, then shielded it again. She programmed in a trigger, one only she could release once she placed the poison memory into her victims.

Then she opened a small, one-way portal into the memory. Into it, she poured her own anger, her own horror, and her own vehemence. She closed the portal, satisfied the small bomb she carried in her head would drive whoever she planted it into madness, beyond even her reach to recover.

Satisfied, she soaped herself and cleansed her body of *Xian's* filth. The pulsing water had slowed to a tattoo whirling around her, cleaning the last of the soap and the revulsion of the Damned.

She would have stayed there for hours, but the aquaguard chimed. *"Warning. Your water quota is approaching. Rinse and step from the shower. The water will stop in thirty seconds."* Tan waited until the last moment, savoring every drop. A warm jet of air blew from a duct outside the shower as she toweled dry. She dressed swiftly, as they had been taught in the Academy, in the Imperial Intelligence uniform hung on the back of the door, stiff and new in its black leather and rigid filament. Outside the bath, her sister waited in complete silence.

Tranquility had a proper conference room, with an onyx conference table and a dozen comfortable chairs, walls of a pleasant pastel. A large video screen dominated an entire wall. Doctor Ho-Bar announced, "I wish to formally protest this interrogation. She may be your student, but she is my patient. I assuredly do not find her fit for duty."

"I am more familiar with Agent Tan's physiology and abilities," intoned Swartz saKhan. "She has recovered sufficiently for this inquiry. I have taken the liberty of bringing in one of my own agents to facilitate her questioning. Tuhnka?"

Her sister. Of course. Father had planned well. Tuhnka would question and probe, secretly following Imperial Intelligence technique. The Commodore and the doctor were there to bear witness that the inquiry had followed the Laws of Angkor Khan. When Tuhnka had finished her part in the theater, she would only have to wait until the doctor declared Tan fit to return to duty. With the information she stripped from Tan's mind during the "inquiry", she would find Tan's plans for winning the competition. Now that Tan had her "bomb" in place, she needed to protect it at all costs until the time was right to destroy her sister. If Tuhnka should find it, Tan's death would follow quickly. Most likely, Tuhnka would make it appear as an accident.

Very well. Father's plan was a fine plan. He hadn't written the rules of the competition, but he was playing the game masterfully. He had exposed Tuhnka as his favorite. Swartz saKhan was giving her, Tan, to her sister to increases Tuhnka's odds.

"Very well, Father," she thought. *"I'll play the part of your plan for today. But I have plans of my own. And abilities not even you suspect. In the end, I shall enjoy watching you go mad from my new little toy."*

Tuhnka tapped a control; the video showed Gyona and Tan on the space jacks, marching across the hull of *Xian*. "Will you confirm this is a true image of you and the Mykonos engineer?" she asked.

"I will confirm that after you answer my question." Tan turned to the Commodore. "Ma'am, this inquiry is being held under the Laws of Angkor Khan, correct?"

Katy nodded. "Then I insist on my Right of Privacy." Tan said. "I am a telepath, as is the Intelligence Master and my sister. By the Law, I insist all telepaths wear a neutralizer to prevent unwarranted examination."

"Come now, Sister, what are you trying to hide?" asked Tuhnka.

Swartz saKhan raised his hand. "The request is not unreasonable," he declared. "And if it makes my agent more comfortable for these proceedings, then by all means, I insist her we honor her request." His face was placid, save for his emerald eyes that bore into hers.

Plans within plans, Father.

Neutralizers were produced and for the next hour Tan was questioned over the events of her collapse on *Xian*. She answered each question with care, sticking to the facts as she recalled. Eventually, Tuhnka asked the question she had been most worried about.

"Tell us, Agent Tan, during the course of your examination of the hull of the *Xian,* you became distressed to the point of disengaging from your space jack unit and fell to the exposed hull. What was it that compelled you to do this?"

"I heard screaming," Tan said. "Long, drawn out cries of terror and pain. I tried to investigate the screams by touching the hull as best I could in the vacuum, to see if I could categorize the messages clearer." It was a lie, she knew. But during her coma, part of her had analyzed the empathic assault. Inwardly she smiled. She had devised a shielding from being overwhelmed. It was a mind trick she wished to keep secret from even the saKhan.

"Did you determine the source of these screams?" asked Katy.

"Yes Commodore," said Tan. "They came from inside *Xian.*"

"Can you describe the screams?" Doctor Ho-Bar asked.

"I can," she said, *sotto voce.* "They were the screams of the Damned."

"Commodore," Tan said, "the mission to raise *Xian* is still viable. Investigating what I heard may prove more difficult. I was unable to determine the number of beings on board the ship. Still, I believe the salvage effort should continue, starting with rising *Xian* to a safer orbit. From there we can plan an investigation of him before salvage begins."

"Agent Tan, you have been in a coma for eight days," Commodore O'Hare said. "While you were unconscious, the *Xian* has been raised to a safe and stable orbit. We have an Imperial Army boarding battalion on hand. The operation to board and secure *Xian* begins in sixteen hours."

Katy tugged at the collar of her uniform jacket. Technically, Rescue and Salvage Services were attached to the Imperial Navy and as a Naval Officer she had kept a uniform for formal occasions. In reality, she hadn't worn her uniform in nearly twenty years. Somewhere along the line, it had clearly shrunk across her bottom and chest.

Jhon must have some secret to storing his uniform. Each crease was razor sharp. The fit, the tailoring…perfect. The very picture of an Imperial Naval officer from the recruiting posters. He struggled to keep from laughing at Katy's dress as she sat on the *Mary Kane's* shuttle, transporting them to the lead troop transport for the briefing of the *Xian*. Protocol demanded that she wear the uniform for the formal meeting with the Army. She would have preferred her working coveralls and sweater. And a wee nip.

"There they are," Jhon announced. "Gah, what ugly beasts."

The three troop carriers were models of efficiency. Fifteen hundred feet long, their hulls were straight oval hulls, two breeching pods attached to the belly of each transport, a small star drive on the upper hull. Each was painted Army green and black, spikey yellow numbering identifying each ship. *"Leave it to the Army,"* mused Katy. *"Fugly ships with no names, just numbers."*

The shuttle swept alongside the lead transport docking port and joined with a shudder. The airlock lights cycled, the hatches opened. Katy followed naval protocol as she boarded the transport, saluting the Army officer who braced at the entryway. "Permission to come aboard," she requested.

"Permission granted Ma'am," he responded. "Welcome aboard *I.A.T. 1042.* Colonel Cavner is waiting for you on the parade deck."

"Very well. Lead on, Major," Katy sighed in in relief. It had been years, but she remembered Army rank tabs.

The parade deck was a large open space aboard the transport, usually used for training personnel. Exercise equipment was today obscured by holos representing the similar parade decks on the other two transports. One hundred soldiers on each ship stood in tight formation. Each soldier wore a modern chameleon combat uniform. The helmets were closed, presenting a carbon grey line of masked, fierce, determined Imperial soldiers. Their weapons were varied, from advanced rail rapid fire weapons to mini howitzers.

As she stepped across the threshold came the order "Attention! Imperial Rescue and Salvage Fleet One, arriving!" As one on all three ships, the soldiers snapped to attention, their weapons held vertical. A tall, cadaverous Army colonel snapped a professional salute, the slightest of quiver as his fingertips touched the brim of his cap adding to the sharpness of his demeanor. Under his hooked nose grew a thick, well-trimmed moustache, matching a pair of heavy brown eyebrows flecked with grey. His eyes were dark, nearly black and squinting, the eyes of a warrior immune to the death and suffering of countless enemies.

The green and black dress uniform was impeccable, of course, a rectangular display of awards on his left breast, the golden Imperial Eagle of his rank gleaming on his collar. "Colonel Daryl

Cavner, Imperial Army Special Forces," he stated. "Sapper unit ODA 1322 standing by for inspection." His voice was a remarkably clear tenor, the voice of a singer contradicting his rugged visage.

Katy returned the salute as she remembered from her Academy days, wrist locked, fingers tight and snapping to the brim of her cap, then hand dropped to her side the next instant, right thumb perfectly aligned with the gold piping on her uniform trousers. She nodded.

"Sah-gent Mah-juh!" called Cavner. "Inspect the troops!"
"SUH!" came the reply. "Sapper unit ODA 1322, Inspect-HUT!"

With a single thump, the three hundred soldiers snapped their rifles at an angle, twisted their heads to the left and opened their helmets. The Terrans' shaved heads shone in the light, along with the polished shells of the dozen Cruestans and the buzz cut fur of the twenty-five Mykonos soldiers. With the Sergeant Major leading, Katy and Colonel Cavner trailing, Katy stopped before each soldier briefly, looking from boots to their faces. The Commodore could see that their faces were as hairless as possible, thereby increasing the efficiency of the scalp connections of their uniforms. For the Mykonos, this meant they had white patches of skin showing through their short fur.

On each soldier's right arm was the record of the individual soldier's combat engagements. The first rows had lists from shoulder to nearly the wrist. The further down the ranks, the lists grew shorter, though no soldier had less than a bicep of battles.

Katy finished her examination, including the holos from the troop ships to the left and right. The inspection party returned to the front of the theater. "A fine-looking team, Colonel," said Katy. "My compliments."

Colonel Cavner answered. "Thank you, Commodore," he said with pride. "Shall we proceed with the briefing?"

With the troop at parade rest, a young captain marched forward and saluted. "Captain William Cavner reporting as ordered," he said crisply.

Katy glanced at the Colonel. "Captain Cavner is my son," he confirmed. "As you see, he has been in thirty-eight engagements. His mother and I are very proud."

The young man's cheeks reddened slightly at his father's praise. Katy noted Captain Cavner was as gaunt as his father, but had green, Asian eyes. *"A Royal descendant?"* she pondered. "You may begin, Captain," she ordered.

A holo of *Xian* appeared. "Soldiers, this is the objective, the former Imperial Super Heavy Carrier *Xian*. The ship was decommissioned more than one hundred years ago and has since filled a variety of civilian roles. As you can see, it has sustained heavy battle damage and there is a large plasma fire in the engineering section that will need to be addressed."

Over the course of the next hour, Captain Cavner highlighted various critical areas of the derelict: main bridge, auxiliary bridge, main computer, launch bays. Teams were assigned, missions laid out. The bridges, the main computer and engineering were highest priority. Captain Cavner himself would seize the main bridge and gain control of the vessel.

The image of *Xian* revealed an unusual feature. On the port side was a circular hole, shards of clearsteel and shattered framework. No light came from the hole. Katy pointed and asked about it.

"The hole is located over a cargo bay," explained Captain Cavner. "We can find no explanation for the window that was there before the battle. We are detecting a high amount of silica and some organic materials. As the bay is open to space and the diagrams doesn't show any value to the space, we are ignoring it until the ship is secure. At that point, a survey team can examine it."

"Thank you, Captain Cavner." His father adjusted the holo, and the *Xian* disappeared. Three figures appeared. "Here is the face of our enemy," he said. "The giant cats appear to be our biggest threat. We've not met them in battle, so I have no advice, save to remember the words of the ancient soldier from Terra; 'He who shoots firstest, fastest and straightest wins.' As soon as you have a shot, clear or not, get rounds on the target. Medical reports the skull is thinner than we would expect, so head shots will be effective. But you'll do well to fire on the body as well.

"These ugly fellows (Captain Cavner's pointer highlighted the second figure,) we're calling the Red Heads, for obvious reasons. The salvage fleet soldiers have engaged them, they haven't been observed with any weapons, but are exceptional at hand to hand combat. They are big and powerful. Dissections have revealed they are of Terran origin, but the majority of their internal organs have been replaced by mechanical components. Body shots will damage them, but it'll take a lot to kill them that way. Their vulnerability is that nice, fat, red head. Their sensory components are there, along with their brain stem and central processor. Head shot will kill the bastards.

"This last group of fellows are the wild card. Postmortems have shown they are Terran, with minor deviancies that can be attributed to environment of their planets of origin and natural selection. It appears they are a slave class. The Red Heads broke their arms and stuffed them into space suits. The environmental controls were found at the lowest possible settings, enough to live and keep the rebreathers working. When the Red Head's air supplies got low, they'd connect with their slave's suit and drain their air supply to survive. The dead slaves were cast adrift.

"This third class was also found in the survival pods with the big cats. Apparently, the cats require a great deal of sustenance to survive. They drug the poor bastards into the survival pods with them and dined on them when they got hungry.

"However, our psychologists have examined the few survivors we have found and determined most of them are supporting their murderous masters rather than their Terran brothers. We can't be sure how they will react when you encounter them. Your standing order for the slaves is to give them a single chance to surrender. If they won't or if they attack, take them out. We don't need them to control or operate *Xian*. Commodore?"

Katy placed her hands on her hips and scanned the hundreds of dark, eager eyes staring unblinking at her. "The *Xian* is presenting us more questions than answers," she told the warriors. "But, in the end, he is nothing more than an obsolete hulk, worthy only of salvage. Protect yourselves and your fellow soldiers at all times."

She raised both hands high above her head and shouted, "For the greater glory of the mighty Terran Empire! For the never-ending glory of our cherished Empress Joaquina Russolov Khan!"

The troops raised their weapons above their heads; officers and ratings on all three ships raised their hands, claws, paws and tentacles and cried, "HooooOOOO! HooooOOOO! HooooOOOO!"

Chapter 13

Precisely one hour later, filled with combat troops and their small crews, the six breeching ships dropped silently away from the troop transports. The least attractive ships of the fleet, each was shaped like an oversized onion, tendrils at the base of the wide bottom of the vessel and a cylindrical command center at the top. Fully loaded, they carried fifty shock troops and all their equipment for boarding a vessel forcibly.

As the ships approached the hulk of the *Xian,* the tendrils at their bases extended and spread. They scanned for the airlocks they had been preprogramed to find, located them and centered the ships over them. The tendrils expanded, forming a boarding skirt. Contact was made with the *Xian's* hull; the skirt ballooned as it filled with a breathable atmosphere. Small motors that ringed the fattest edge of the ship fired, holding the inflated bubble firmly against the hull of the derelict, the pressurized skirt a necessary precaution. In the event the pirates who had stolen *Xian* had booby trapped the airlock, the skirt was frangible. It could absorb the explosion or tear away, protecting the valuable breach ship and its precious cargo.

A probe extended to the airlock door. It deployed a narrow drilling laser, barely the width of a hair. Once it had cut through the door, a second hair-thin probe penetrated the hole and sniffed the atmosphere inside the airlock.

"High traces of carbon," announced the technician operating the sensor probe. "Radiation a bit high, as we might expect. Some other inert gasses. Lots of methane, but not a dangerous level."

"Sappers cleared to the airlock." The order came from five of the ships. On the sixth, a vacuum was found beyond the *Xian's* airlock door, making entry there impractical. The breeching ship backed away and moved on to its secondary target. This airlock was acceptable, so the sappers went to work there as well.

The exterior doors opened, using *Xian's* own manual controls. The sapper pairs, at work on the interior doors, repeated the survey of the passage beyond the airlock using the same laser drill and sample tube. Satisfied, they opened the panels containing the circuitry operating the airlocks and installed their own controls. Four soldiers, their chameleon armor activated, entered the airlock and stood ready by the sides of the hatch. Sappers finished, and inner hatches opened, the soldiers entered the passageway with caution, only moving down the hallway when more soldiers appeared from the breech ship.

In this fashion, three hundred Imperial shock troops boarded *Xian* in minutes. The airlocks were closed, and the breeching ships moved off. Shuttles from Katy's recovery fleet moved in, attaching external airlocks and docking ports. Until the soldiers could secure one of the three remaining docking arms, this would be the only way to safely board and exit *Xian.*

"Kami three to Kami actual. We've taken up positions at the bridge and are ready to take it down," Captain Cavner reported to his father.

"Kami actual to Kami three, execute. Good hunting, son," Colonel Cavner answered.

Captain Cavner took a deep breath, releasing it slowly, willing himself to relax. It was always just like this, just before battle. His senses were razor sharp, his body a cobra, poised to strike. He had trained his team well. They were fit, ready and eager. "Kami three to Kami squad. Ingress in three, two, one, execute!"

Small charges exploded, forcing the doors open. The surprise was complete as twenty-five Imperial soldiers, camouflaged by third generation chameleon armor, raced into the room. The thirty-six slaves who had taken terrified refuge in the bridge startled as they were confronted by nearly invisible wraiths storming through the doors and into their midst. Orders telling them to drop to the floor were obeyed by few, but most stood in terror, unsure what was happening. Two slaves charged the wraiths and were gunned down before they could take two steps.

On seeing their brethren die, fifteen of the slaves dropped to the floor, blubbering. The remaining who stood were dispatched by accurate and unmerciful Imperial fire.

William opened his comm back to his father's ship. "Kami three actual to Kami six actual," he reported. "Operation a success. We have the bridge. *Xian* is ours."

The five other teams reported success with their boarding of the *Xian*. One hundred seventy slaves had surrendered, nearly two hundred either panicked and tried to flee or attacked the boarding parties. Unarmed, they stood no chance.

Sergeant Gordo Freeman led two privates from the landing at the auxiliary toward Engineering. His assignment was to make sure the passage was clear of enemies and ensure the hallway was clear of any entanglements. He hated the mission. The engineers from the fleet hadn't arrived and repaired the starboard reactors, so the light in the corridor was flashing on and off. The optics of his battle armor adjusted automatically, but it was distracting. He had arrived aboard on the second wave leaving the breeching ship, so all the shooting was over by the time he got aboard. Still, he fingered the trigger of his rail weapon. Since the colonel had described the enemies they were likely to face, he had been eager to engage the space pirates who had stolen this ship. He wanted one of the enormous cat creature that looked fearsome and nearly impossible for a single soldier to take down. Well, he'd do it! Big creatures didn't faze him; the bigger the better! Either he'd fill the damn thing full of expanding memory metal slugs that tore flesh and smashed bone or he'd die when the beast engulfed him, die with his trigger on full auto and demolishing his enemy.

The map on his faceplate indicated an intersection with one of the primary passages that ran the length of *Xian*. He motioned orders to the privates behind him; one on either wall of this passageway, the man across from him to check the main behind him while he checked the other. The third soldier would back the two of them up, should there be any trouble.

The lights dropped off. Power to this section was out. The night vision scopes on his helmet strained to see anything in the absolute darkness.

He removed the sneak sphere from his belt and tossed it around the corner. It activated as it fell, stopping a foot above the floor. The tiny drone sent rough images back to Freeman's helmet, while moving slowly down the hallway. In the low light with the sneak's limited sensors, Sergeant Freeman couldn't make out details of the passage. There was no movement, but the walls looked odd. Misshapen columns hung from above. They were arranged in pairs, each pair approximately four feet apart. He signaled the private across from him, who shook his head and raised his hand, palm up with a shrug. Gordo interfaced with Private Hammonds sneak. It was showing the same odd pair of columns every four feet.

Gordo pointed to the passageway and held up five fingers. He counted down, one finger at a time. On the closed fist, both warriors swung around in the main passageway, weapons lowered and ready to fire. The third soldier stood behind the corner, ready to assist if either of his comrades encountered trouble.

The lights returned suddenly. Gordo startled, partially from the light, from the image of hundreds of naked men, hung by harnesses every four feet the length of the passageway as far as he could see. Their heads were upright, their eyes staring forward, unblinking. Hair and beards hung in long mats from their sagging faces. The bodies hung limp. Feces and urine stained their legs and puddled beneath each man.

As if on cue and in unison, all of them inhaled through gaping mouths together, then exhaled.

Gordo could hear small noises from his comm, gagging and weeping. "Wha-wha-what the *frack*, Sarge?" One of the privates must have opened his helmet, for the sound of puking resounded in the dead quiet area. Nearly thirty years in the army hadn't prepared Gordo for anything like this. The inhale and the exhale happened again, in unison. He couldn't help himself; he felt himself pissing at the sight of an endless line of hanging men breathing together.

Sergeant Gordo Freeman, Imperial Army, always preached to stick to your training. Faced with two endless rows fore and aft of…zombies was the only word he could think of. He had to report in! He opened his comm and call out "Medic! Medic needed on deck six, intersection twenty-one bravo. Medic, Medics. Shit, Lots of medics. Now! Hurry!"

The calls for medics were coming from all thirty teams aboard the *Xian*. Daryl Cavner, warrior, survivor of over two hundred fifty encounters with dozens of enemies didn't hesitate. "Commodore, I need all three hospital ships." His voice was calm. "I'm going to order my teams to complete their surveys of the primary passageways of *Xian* and keep a running tally of whatever casualties are they are reporting."

"I'll reposition *Mercy* to *Xian* until we have a better idea of what we're facing," Katy responded. "I'll have Doctor Ho-Bar shuttle here to direct the triage. Can your soldiers send us an image so we can see what we're dealing with?"

Within moments, a holo-image appeared, taken from the sensors of a soldier's helmet. The evocative appearance of a stupefied male hanging slacked faced and soiled. On cue, he inhaled and exhaled with his fellow prisoners. Vacant eyes didn't react when the hallway lights illuminated.

"I'll add the *Tranquility,*" said Katy. "And have *Repose* standing by."

"We have Engineering secured, Ma'am," said the Colonel. "May I suggest getting the engineering team aboard immediately to start working the burning reactors? All this effort will be moot if we don't get those fires under control."

"Agreed," said Katy. "I'll return to *Mary Kane* and co-ordinate the salvage from there. We'll also put a team to work seeing if we can get a shuttle bay operating. We can operate a triage easier from there than trying to work through the smaller airlocks. You are to continue securing the ship. Take prisoners if possible, but your soldiers are to protect themselves at all times. Shoot first, we can sort the details later."

The Commodore took a last look at the image of the vacant eyed, slack jawed prisoner. Her mouth was suddenly very dry.

Chapter 14

Of the many lessons Katy O'Hare learned in the Academy decades ago, she found the art of delegation the most useful. It had served her well as she ascended in her naval career. As Commodore of an Imperial salvage fleet, the talent was irreplaceable. Even the salvage of a damaged freighter or a dead star fighter took teamwork and Katy was forever grateful to her instructors and mentors over the years who taught her how to let the right people do their jobs.

Today found her touring *Xian* with her experts: propulsion and structural engineers, electronic technicians, medical doctors and of course, Colonel Cavner and his son. The team started in Engineering where her own Chief Engineer, Dan Diezac, was directing the effort. "I took the liberty of commandeering the processing engineer from the *Solarius Maru*," he explained. "Radford Hembree has been working with breeder reactors for forty years and is best suited for the fires onboard. Radford?"

Radford Hembree was raised in the desert plains of west Texas on Terra, in a family of roughnecks. While petroleum no longer was a useful energy source, other markets for oil existed. The Hembree family name was famous (some would suggest infamous) throughout Occident for hard drinking, hard fighting and hardworking men and women who took energy production as a family vocation. Radford graduated at the top of his class in University. His name got him a hundred job offers. His brilliance made him a wealthy man. Diezac had played on his pride and patriotism after Hembree turned sixty, almost dared him to work with the salvage fleet. Never one to shy from a challenge, the billionaire had enthusiastically accepted the job.

He pulled a grimy gauntlet off his right hand and extended it to Katy. "Pleased to meet you, Ma'am," his accent pure Texas. In his teeth, a fat cigar wafted smoke about his grey hair.

"Er, pleased to meet you, Mister Hembree," Katy said. "You'll excuse me, but is that tobacco? You do know that's illegal across the Empire."

Hembree retracted his offered hand, taking the cigar instead and waving its vile smell around. "Way I figger, the Empire is two or three light years that-a-away," he said, pointing aft. "Seein' how we're not in the Empire, the question of the legality of my *cee-gar* is a moot point, ain't it, Commodore?"

He chomped back his on his cigar and drawled, "Aw-right, let's git to work, shall we? What we got here is a pretty interesting setup. Five breeder reactors set up in series to process gases the collection gigs bring in. The gasses travel through the extracting the lighter elements first, then on to the heaviest in the final stage. In each case, the process gasses are cooled and stored cryogenically to make them easier to handle. Nice little setup, state of the art fifty, seventy-five years ago.

"Pretty obvious what happened. First, whoever was operating the system didn't know diddly about how to set it up or work it. The valves were in a cockamamie arrangement that sent processed gasses back into the system or vented out into space. Hence, they collected very little fuel or usable gasses. Secondly, they didn't seem to understand just how carefully you have to run a system like this. The blown-up docking bay is the biggest piece of evidence.

"They had someone get sloppy there. Either bad piloting or the hookup with a collection ship was wrong. Either way, that's where the first explosion took place. The force of the explosion followed the gas paths through the holding tanks, over pressurizing them. They vented like they're supposed to, through the reactors. That's where their screwy valve setup doomed them. Instead of a nice, sequential opening of the relief valves across the whole reactor system, the surge blew out the first two banks of reactors. That's the fire we're seeing, ten reactors venting unprocessed gas and igniting with the heat of the reactors. Fortunately, these reactors are allowing the gas to vent. Unfortunately, once the raw storage tanks are empty, the reactors will start burning off themselves. When that happens, you won't have to worry about salvaging ol' *Xian.* The biggest chunk of her will be about the size of a chigger bug."

"So the *Xian* is a lost cause," said Katy. "I should evacuate my personnel and push her in a direction where her detonation will cause the least harm?"

"Nah, that was the bad news," explained Hembree. "The good news is all the reactors are modular. When they built this system, they planned for this kind of an accident. The reactors can be disconnected and jettisoned easily enough, except it'll take some time. There's the rub. The book says we need forty hours per reactor. But I figger we ain't got but one hundred thirty, hundred forty hours left before the reactors go critical and start exploding.

"I have a plan. I'll need purt near every engineer working double shifts. Lucky us again, the radiation in the vessel containment rooms is relatively low. They're still gonna need a regen nap is the hospital for two days, but they'll be ready to go when they come out. It comes down to numbers, Commodore. We can save the ship for you to drag off to the scrappers or we can shoot her on a course away from here and let physics take their course."

"No mention of the civilians hung in the passageways," thought Katy. *"Good, we've kept that compartmentalized."*

"Start the process for jettisoning the reactors," Katy ordered. "Dan, co-ordinate through *Mary Kane*, pull every engineer the fleet can spare. I'm inclined, for now, to save this ship for salvage rather than simply writing him off."

Katy returned to her shuttle. While she could have easily made the mile-long journey walking to her next meeting, Colonel Cavner had objected. "We haven't completely secured the vessel," he announced. "I won't have a flag officer wandering the halls until I know it's safe." He had also seen the images of the victims.

The trip from the engineering airlock to the bridge took seconds. Captain Cavner had arranged an honor guard for her, troops in battle armor lining her journey to the bridge. His father was there with his staff, along with Doctor Ho-Bar and several medical officers. "Ship's status," snapped Katy, all business, ready to start her tour.

Colonel Cavner started. Waving his arm around the bridge, he said, "All this is useless. Whoever was running this vessel cut off all connections or smashed all necessary equipment. We've got lots of pretty, shiny lights, but that's it. Same in Auxiliary Control. The ship's computer has locked up, that's why the lighting is intermittent throughout the ship. Engineer Diezac assures me he can repair Auxiliary Control. So, when he's finished, we'll have limited control over *Xian*. I would also suggest we install one of our own computers and secure this ship's computer in case the enemy left us any more surprises."

"Agreed. Take charge, Colonel," said Katy. "Medical?"

"We've counted nearly eleven thousand of the victims," said Ho-Bar. "We have indications there may be several thousand more. They are linked through a foreign implement that has been inserted into their brain stem. Each of these…spikes, have sent filaments connecting to nearly every neural connection in the brain. Fascinating, really, the information in and out of the brain in via a direct connection. Something somewhere is controlling every aspect of each being. Pulse, respiration, the endergonic secretions, all being controlled by a single source."

"Are they alive?" asked Katy.

"Difficult to say," Ho-Bar answered. "We tried removing the spike from one victims head. As soon as the spike and its filaments were removed, the patient died immediately. Same thing when we tried disconnecting the wiring harness from the spike. Instant death. We tried removing, then immediately reattaching the wiring, but to no avail. The victim immediately dies.

"We hooked up an electro cranial web to examine brain waves and patterns. The dominate patterns were identical, control signals sent via the spike. Secondary indications on most of the remaining victims are flat lined. Those I would say are dead."

"The rest?" asked Katy.

Ho-bar touched a control on the medical sensor on his belt. It projected holo after holo of slack, blank faces. "You can't tell just looking," he said. "As many as thirty-five to forty percent are showing signs of consciousness. Perhaps even rational thought." He swallowed and said hoarsely, "There are signs they are being tortured. The indications I am reading show they are suffering horribly."

The room went silent as face after blank face was displayed. "One more curiosity, Commodore," The holo expanded, showing the full image of the complete body, head to toe. "All the victims are male," said Doctor Ho-Bar. "No females. None. The colonies that were raided had thousands of women, adult and children. There were bodies left behind, of course. But not the thousands we would expect. Roughly fifty one percent of all the population of the raided colonies were women. Where did the women all go?"

"I believe we have the beings on hand who would know," Katy said. "In addition, the condition of the victims appears to be deteriorating since we boarded. Colonel, I want the medical personnel from the slave population culled out and questioned. The women are somewhere on this ship. For the rest, I will offer parole for the duration of the situation until I decide the final disposition of the *Xian* and her crew.

"The operation for jettisoning the burning reactors has started. Within one hundred twenty hours, we will know for certain as to whether this ship is salvageable of not. I want answers for the victims before that."

"Commodore, can we get some of the telepaths to assist us?" asked Colonel Cavner. "It would more efficient if we knew which victims are still alive should we be forced to evacuate."

"I will approach Intelligence Master Swartz on the matter," Katy agreed. "Unfortunately, he's already had one agent injured when in close contact with this vessel. Anything else?"

They all shook their heads. "Very well, then," Katy ordered. "Let's get to work.

Two thousand male colonists had survived the raids on the colonies. For reasons known only to their captors, these survivors were enslaved, stripped and forced to wear the blue shorts and boots that identified them as slaves. Theirs were the unpleasant toils demanded by their masters, the cleaning and care of their cargo and performing the menial tasks. Beatings and starvation had winnowed their number below twelve hundred.

Physicians were in high demand. Thirty thousand captives needed to be kept healthy as possible for the journey home. While losses were to be expected, woe be to the physician-slaves who allowed any under their care to die unnecessarily. At best, the Red Heads would beat them to death. At worst, they would receive the spike and be hung in storage.

Those who survived the Imperial boarding had been imprisoned in a large cargo holding. No food, little water was provided. Most of the slaves fell into the stupor of despair, huddled together or curled into balls scattered around the chamber. No one spoke to any of the others. The Masters had demanded silence and were prone to beating or hanging a disobedient slave. Now that the Imperials were their Masters, they saw no reason to consider otherwise. Indeed, in their previous lives, many had fled the Empire, seeking a perceived freedom from the Empire and its Law. To have survived one master and be handed over to another was too much to bear.

"Attention!" came a call over the tannoy. "Attention to the slaves of the *Xian*!" (Ah, that was the name of their ship. Until now, none had been told this tidbit of information.) "By the Laws of Angkor Khan and the regulations of the Imperial Navy and Army, you are now considered Imperial Slaves. As such, food and water will be provided for you shortly. The Commodore, in her magnanimous mercy, has offered parole for all slaves who agree to return to their duties caring for the victims of the crimes inflicted upon them by you and your previous masters. As the Law states: "Work and be fed." Should any of you refuse this parole, she has rendered judgment on your crimes and has ordered restrained spacing, so your bodies may be recycled.

"First, I require all physicians accepting parole to stand and form a line at the portal."

Sixty survivors made their way to their feet and shuffled to the doorway where they were escorted out by the wraith-guards.

"Very good. Now the rest of you. If you accept the Commodore's generous offer of parole, stand on your feet. You will be taken to a place where you may clean yourselves and be fed. Then you will be sent about on your duties." Over one thousand of the slaves struggled to their feet and shuffled to the open door. Seventy of their companions stayed huddled on the deck, too terrified, too tired or too defiant to move.

"You have disobeyed an order by the Commodore. As slaves, your sentence is death." Squads of the wraiths streamed in bearing zip cuffs and chain. The slaves' hands were bound behind their backs, chains were looped around their waists in groups of ten. A few stayed on the floor, refusing to move. Their hair was grabbed by the guards' gauntleted hands and they were dragged to the nearest airlocks.

Slaves began to plead for their lives as each string of ten was thrust into the execution chamber. After ten minutes, when the entire chain was dead, the outer hatch was sealed. Twice, the slaves resisted, desperate to escape their fate. It proved futile; nude, starving and tired slaves against crack Imperial Shock Troops.

"How much longer, Sergeant?" asked the details officer, a young lieutenant with only two dozen combat stripes on her sleeve.

"Hmmmm," the Sergeant replied. "Half hour? Forty minutes? Give or take. Why, you got a hot date, Lieutenant?"

"Nah, I'm just getting a little hungry," said the young officer. "They just reopened the officer's mess. Like to see what kind of lunch they scraped up."

Chapter 15

"Let me get this straight, Commodore," Swartz's green eyes narrowed. "You are asking me to place my most experienced and senior agents in a situation that might very well damage them at the very least and drive them mad at the very worst. And you're asking me to order them to do this. We've seen the effect on Agent Tan, now you wish for me to expose Agent Tuhnka."

The temperature of the conference room aboard the *Loki* seemed to drop twenty degrees. His daughters, Tan and Tuhnka, sat to either side of the conference table wearing Imperial Intelligence black uniforms, their hands folded on the table. Both Tan's ink black and Tuhnka's shimmering gold hair was pulled back tightly like a helmet. Their black eyes stared inscrutably at Katy O'Hare.

"I am most certainly not ordering any of your agents to board *Xian*," explained Katy. "Agent Tan is a valued member of my staff. I deeply regret her injuries and would not be asking her to attempt this mission if there were any other choice. We have one hundred twenty hours before the burning reactors on *Xian* begin to feed on themselves and destroy the ship. Doctor Ho-Bar's staff is working on a method to detach any surviving victims from the life support net they are connected to. But, setting up the brain scan unit to check to see if they are still viable takes time. Should we be forced to evacuate, I fear we may be forced to leave some potential survivors behind."

"Have you so little faith in Engineer's Diezac's abilities?" asked Tan. "I've worked alongside him for two years and have found him to be an outstanding engineer. Am I to understand he is not capable of this task?"

"Physics don't care about ability," shot back Katy. "Engineer Diezac is more than capable to the task and he has pulled in every asset available to save *Xian*. It may not be enough."

"So there is the possibility he will succeed."

"Absolutely," the Commodore answered. "Engineers Diezac and Hembree are our best chance at maintaining *Xian* until we can rescue the surviving victims. Having your agents assist Doctor Ho-Bar will prepare us for any event."

"What about the missing women?" asked Tuhnka. "I understand that you haven't found any of them so far. What are you doing for them?"

"I've enlisted the aid of the surviving slaves," explained Katy. "Given they are trained for this work, it makes the most sense. Additionally, we found a substantial number of physician slaves trained in the care of the colonists. I anticipate many were involved caring for the women; they will lead us to them straightaway. I've also ordered Colonel Cavner and his troops to continue searching the *Xian.*" If they are anywhere on board, I am confident we will find them."

"It is of the utmost importance you find the women," demanded Tuhnka. "You must use every resource to find them, even at the expense of the male captives!"

"Daughter!" exploded Swartz in mindspeak. "You say too much! You will be silent!"

"Father, if my investigation is correct, we must find the females before the Crown Prince and his Battlegroup arrive," Tuhnka replied. "We know the Sudahar wish to expand to this sector. That their lackeys and slaves are here, now, on this ship proves my theory. You must acknowledge the facts."

"I see no facts, Tuhnka, only your suppositions and fears," her father said. "The only facts I see is a derelict ship this *Homo Sapiens is* trying to salvage and its contents of even more *Homo Sapiens.* What is the death of a few thousand more of our inferiors, anyway? One day, when the war comes between the *Homo Sapiens* and the *Homo Superior,* these deaths will be inconsequential. We will be slaying them by the billions."

"Father, may I offer a solution?" Tan interrupted. "While I was incapacitated following my incident with the *Xian,* my subconscious created a natural block containing the memories of what attacked me. When Tuhnka called to me and pulled me back, I believe she extracted me from this module. In meditation, I have examined the block and reinforced it with a stronger shielding. I have examined the memories already stored within the element and strengthened the shield to prevent them from escaping. I have also added a port where new memories can be stored and categorized. I used a virus methodology to create it, therefore I believe I can reproduce it and place it in Tuhnka's mind as well, so she will be protected from the Xian's captives."

"Directly into my brain? Oh, I think not, Sister," Tuhnka objected. "Just the weak brand of attack I would expect from the second-rate likes of you. Truly, my Father extracted your DNA from a hapless streetwalker from a ghetto world, unlike my own superior breeding. How fortunate for you Father has not yet released me from his order to restrain myself from killing you. Did you honestly believe I am going to allow you to plant something into my superior brain that will stay me from my mission?"

"I had rather hoped so." Tan's response dripped with sarcasm. "Do you really think I am clever enough to do that to you, dear sister? Perhaps you are not as formidable as Father believes if you are this frightened of me."

"Enough!" Swartz's order cut through the argument. "Tan, give it to me. I will examine it and if it is all you say it is, then I shall place it in Tuhnka. Then you two will board *Xian* and aid the inferiors in their search. Should you yield positive results, I shall have the module placed in more agents' minds to accelerate the search. Move quickly; keep in mind the females are our target. We must find them, understood?"

"Yes, Father," the obedient agents said. Tan duplicated her mental device, careful to conceal the glee she felt deep in her protected center. Father was allowing his hubris to blind him from her superiority over Tuhnka. That he was taking her "bomb" himself…she wanted to leap and dance about with joy. Soon, oh so very soon she would be the *na-Sahn,* Intelligence Master of the Empire. Oh, she'd grieve her dead sisters, as was the matter of course after such a deed was accomplished. And she'd make sure her dear, poor father was kept protected, and silent, in his madness as he faded and eventually died from her bomb.

The silent conversation had taken five long seconds.

"Very well, Commodore," Swartz said. "My agents will require an hour meditation to prepare. When they are ready, I shall have them transported to *Xian* to assist Doctor Ho-Bar. Is that all?"

"Just this." Katy pulled a spike from her pocket. It was six inches long, tapered chrome. Fine fibers hung from the smooth sides like fringe. "This is the device the pirates used to control the colonists," she explained. "When the med teams extracted it, the unit shut down and the patient died. I'd like your technicians to examine it and see what they can find."

Swartz held the device with two fingers. *Interesting,* he thought. *A means to control the inferiors without having to actually sully one's self by touching their filthy, primitive minds. Could this be used as a weapon?* "I shall send it to our laboratory for inspection. Perhaps we can find the answers for your physicians. If that is all, Commodore, my agents need to retire to their meditations and I have my duties to attend to," he said, rising. "As I'm sure you do, as well."

Damari Russell had, as he liked to say, *survived* the mean streets of South Chicago on Terra. He had always been small, scrawny, with a head full of dreadlocks. It was their culture, his mother would explain. His father had worn dreads. So had both his grandfathers. As far back as anyone could remember, the Russell men wore the dreads of the faithful from the motherland.

As a small child, he learned quickly that if he were to survive, he was going to need to rely on his quickness and smarts instead of brute force. Knowledge would be his weapon and with it he would escape Chicago. And Terra.

He saw what his future would be if he stayed in the neighborhood. As a child, several of his classmates were caught stealing. They would return from police custody with caning marks across their backs. Each time they were caught, there would be more scars than the last time. Most learned to quit stealing. A few never learned their lesson. A dozen one-handed former thieves lived in their neighborhood of decrepit buildings. One or two thieves who tried crime again wore hoods when they went out, to hide the hideous "T" branded on their foreheads.

He, his mama and five brothers and sisters lived in a four-room apartment with peeling wallpaper. He had never met his father. Mama worked twelve hours a day in a local factory sewing Imperial Army uniforms. His older brother was a civil servant, working the nightshift cleaning the streets.

Damari's hard work was rewarded. At eighteen, instead of being pressed into civil service like his brother, or the military,

Damari found himself off to college to study engineering. He met Dan Diezac during a symposium on autonomous circuitry repair and each left an impression on the other. At graduation, Damari had his choice of hundreds of corporate jobs. Instead, he accepted a job to work under his mentor in the Imperial Salvage Fleet. At twenty-two, Damari Russell escaped Chicago and travelled to the stars.

Fifteen years later, he was assistant Chief Engineer on the Imperial tug *Tatoosh*. The Chief was expected to retire soon; Damari was there to learn the ship and take over as soon as the old Chief retired.

Today, he was on the rescue mission of the *Xian*. An odd circuit was drawing a lot of energy from the principle reactor. As power should have been premium on *Xian,* an unknown circuit taking that much power continuously warranted investigation. He grabbed a hand sensor and tool kit and proceeded through the maze of *Xian's* passageways. Several times he stopped, unfolded the portable ladder he carried in his back pocket and examine the circuit visually in the overhead. The gauge of the wire seemed to be far too light for the amount of power it was carrying. Nevertheless, it showed no sign of overheating or failing.

Frustrated, he pulled off his watch cap, gave his scalp a good scratch and re-donned the grey neo-wool head covering. The circuit made no sense to the well-organized engineer. The trail was leading him into an unsecured section of the *Xian*. The lights snapped off and on with a maddening irregularity. Environmental control was malfunctioning, too. One minute he pulled his jacket tightly, wishing he had worn something heavier, the next minute the temperature would soar. Gravity would grind him down to the point of crawling, and then his head was bouncing off the ceiling.

He stumbled across an Army patrol, not seeing them because of their chameleon armor. They questioned him briefly, then gave him a beacon to clip to his belt. "If you run into trouble, activate the beacon," the soldier voice was a mechanical clatter. "We'll be there in less than five minutes. Good luck." The wraith-like soldiers faded away as the cadre moved down the hallway.

The sensor led him to a pair of nondescript doors at the end of a short hallway. The power feed he was following led through those doors and the room beyond showed an abundance of power. He debated calling Dan Diezac but decided to investigate for himself first.

The hallway went dark again. Damari held a small flashlight in his teeth as he removed the keypad lock from the wall. Twice he stopped, hearing thumps behind him. He shone his larger flashlight up the hallway behind him, the second time retreating back up to the intersection that he'd turned down this passageway. He heard faint tapping and the scurrying of tiny feet. *Rats. Grobfelbing rats, just like back home in Chicago.* He chuckled to himself. You could take the boy from the ghetto, but the ghetto would always be part of the boy.

Back at the keypad, the ripper he used was of his own design, used terabytes of information and could open any lock up to seventy characters in seconds. It was highly illegal, so he was careful to use a standard Imperial casing and kept it out of sight whenever Intelligence was about.

After ten minutes, the little box flashed a red light and made an unhappy quacking noise. Damari was stunned, nearly dropping his valuable ripper. It couldn't figure out the combination! That had never happened before!

He pulled the old-fashioned crowbar from his backpack. He had always boasted about being the "skinniest three-hundred-pound black man you'll ever meet." Today, his wiry strength, aided by the four-foot crowbar, saved the day. He grunted and strained, nearly to the point of surrendering and calling for help, when the doors opened with a low, mournful groan.

A wave of heat rolled through the opening, pulling a yellow fog through the door and down the passageway. Damari jumped back but was quickly engulfed by the scorching mist that smelled of citrus. He stripped his backpack and jacket, retaining his scanner and at the last second, his trusty crowbar. The level of the mist had sunk to waist deep, revealing a tub, four feet high, four wide and six deep. He widened the scan to cover the whole, gloomy room. The scanner revealed the room to be one hundred yards long and half as wide. He tightened the focus, eighty of the tubs in the room.

As the mist dropped to his knees, his scanner showed the power to the room increasing. It was the odd thrumming noise he had heard in the passageway, multiplied. More mist poured into the room, venting out the open doors behind him.

Damari aimed his scanner back at the tub directly in front of him and swept its contents.

Life. There was a life form in the tub. He widened his scan field. Currently, excluding himself, his scanner showed eight hundred and twenty life forms. One of the life forms was headed directly towards him. He hefted his trusty crowbar.

"Who is it? Who is there?" The voice was guttural, accented. His translator struggled with the angry voice of the alien. It appeared from the mist, a human slave in blue shorts and boots, wearing a clear plastic coverall. It spied Damari and hurried toward him, then froze.

"Master!" it exclaimed. "This is not an area you are cleared for. Please, I must insist you leave the facility immediately. The cargo is exceedingly fragile and sensitive to external contamination."

"Fragile, my ass!" Said Damari. "What is in these tubs that is so damn fragile and needs so damned much power? Show me."

"Master, please. I cannot," pleaded the slave. "Our current masters ordered us to return to our duties and we have. Ours is the responsibility for the care of the cargo. We are doing our best with the delicate creatures until our director returns. Now, truly, I must insist you leave."

"Not until I see what's taking up so damned much energy," said Damari. "Now, you gonna clear that mist shit out of my way or do I have to dig around and figger it out myself?" Not that he would be able to, what with manipulating the sensor with one hand while holding off the slave with the crowbar in his other.

"As you wish, Master," said the slave. "But only for a moment, as I will have to start decontamination on the cargo as soon as you leave, anyway." The slave, half again as big as Damari, meekly moved to the far end of the tub and began manipulating controls. The mist swirled, then drew into the side of the tub. As its contents came into view, Damari gasped, swayed, retched and jabbed the button on the soldiers' beacon, praying they would be there in less than the five minutes promised.

It was a Terran woman. Or what remained of a Terran woman. Her legs had been removed mid-thigh, her arms just below the shoulder. Her hair was gone, her eyes sutured closed. A mask covered her nose and mouth, a hose ran into her throat. She wasn't breathing that Damari could see and her skin was ghastly white, like a corpse. More wires and tubes connected to various parts of her body. *She must be alive,* Damari thought, at the sight of the nubs of her arms and legs. They twitched, rhythmically.

And she was clearly pregnant.

Chapter 16

The holo snapped and popped as the device strained to resolve the signal. Despite all the resources of Imperial Intelligence, no one had yet been able to come up with a way to beam a clean hologram through otherspace and into regular space.

Tan's heart skipped a beat as the Crown Prince shimmered and resolved. Abdul was tall, dark haired, swarthy and handsome. His emerald eyes bored into her. Tan felt her knees buckle slightly and wavered minutely in a swoon. So long since she had seen him! So long since they…touched. She kowtowed, as was expected with a Crown Prince and chanted, "I greet you, Crown Prince Abdul ab Russolov Khan." She hesitated, then added, "Beloved."

"Tan, my love," he answered. "Apart, but never parted. Have you news for me?"

"Indeed, my Lord," she answered. "I have just been informed in the last hour the nursery has been located. My informants don't have exact numbers, yet. Conservatively, I would say between four and eight thousand incubators in operation."

"And the rest of the colonists?"

"The males have been stored as we hypothesized. Given the known appetites of the feline species, I estimate there are, or were one hundred fifty of them aboard. As for the rest of the females, we are continuing the search. Given the condition of the incubators, though, I suggest we will find them either converted already or in some form of long term storage."

"The *Xian*?" he asked. "Will it be repaired sufficiently to move to my laboratory on Maninquez or should I anticipate securing whatever survivors we can and allowing the remainder to expire when the *Xian* is destroyed?"

"The engineers are hard at work removing the burning reactors," she said. "I have sent surrogates to observe and motivate. The *Sapiens* appear to be responding positively. I will know more within one hundred hours. At that time, either they will be within the period to rescue *Xian*...or forced to start the evacuation. I will contact you when the decision is made."

"The Commodore? Do you have her under control?"

"Difficult to say. Her drinking has increased. This should be compromising her natural defenses. However, she is formidable for a *Sapiens*. I can still influence her, but actual control over her is impossible," reported Tan. "Should *Xian* survive, I am certain she will turn the vessel over to you. In spite of her record, Commodore O'Hare is a loyal officer and a solid citizen. If we present your plan as a benefit to the Empire, she will be certain to aid us. Should the salvage of *Xian* fail, she will be concerned with safely evacuating her crew. She will likely allow us to "rescue" as many of the "poor victims" as we can. However, we have not yet ascertained how to safely disconnect the colonists from *Xian*."

"My late uncle, the Warlord Dakota na-Khan used to say, 'Solve each problem as it presents itself, then move on to the next one,'" quoted the Crown Prince. "Focus on the engineers; see to it they find a way to save Xian. What of your father and sister?"

"I have set my trap, my Lord," she said. "Before you arrive, my sister will be dead, and my father will need me more than ever. Sadly, he will start to deteriorate and will soon be incompetent to run Intelligence. I will humbly accept the position of Intelligence Master until my remaining sisters and I meet. Three are already mine; their bonds of loyalty are unbreakable. The fourth will join us or suffer the same fate of my sister."

"And I will convince my mother to name you sa-Kahn," said the Crown Prince. "Then, when she dies, one of our children will be named my replacement. My useless wife will die soon afterwards from an accident. None will question the legitimacy of our heir children. The Silver line will be cast out and the Black shall once again enter the fold of the heirs!"

"May it be so, Emperor Abdul ab Russolov Khan!" Tan said fervently, kowtowing lower than before. Her black eyes filled with tears of rapturous joy. "May you rule for ten thousand years!"

It was suppertime for Intelligence Master Swartz sa-Khan. He took his meal as he always did, in the privacy of his office. The student agent delivered his meal off a trolley. Her hands were shaking and not from serving the sa-Khan. It was just one of many duties a student honored to serve on the *Loki* could be expected to do. Her shaking was the result of the addition to the wall of his office, across from his desk.

"Control, Child," he instructed the teen girl. "**The shaking of your hands and sweat on your lip tells me your control is slipping. What is unnerving you so?**"

"The man on your wall, Sir," she said. "**He is frightening, filthy and disgusting. I cannot meet his eye, he, he torments me.**"

"He is simply a *Sapiens*," he said. "**An animal, nothing more. He and his kind are who you are destined to rule over one day. Do not concern yourself with him any more than you would a dog or a *cherbart*.**"

"Yes, Master."

He watched her relax, and then gaze at the man pinned to his wall. "**He does look rather foolish and worthless, doesn't he?**" she giggled.

"**When our war is over one day, he and his kind will all be our slaves,**" he said. "**Go now, child, attend to your studies.**"

The teen kowtowed and left, without glancing again at Swartz's prisoner.

The Intelligence Master ate supper while reading reports. His agents on the *Xian,* led by his daughters, were making outstanding progress on the male *Homo Sapiens.* He had approved Tan transferring her shielded virus into the agents, so they could work unencumbered by the mental assault from the tormented beings. Tuhnka had refused to allow Tan to insert the virus into her head directly, so he had done so, after allowing Tuhnka into his mind to examine it. As expected, it had greatly reduced the amount of time needed to determine whether each *Sapiens* was salvageable or not.

The thing on his wall began to make gagging and moaning noises. "You will remain silent," he instructed, deadening the nerves in the thing's throat, "until I have finished my supper." The *Sapiens* had no choice, of course. The method had been developed by Swartz's many times great grandfather, Intelligence Master Noire na-Khan, more than five hundred years before. The subject stood, back against the wall, arms stretched wide. No restraints were necessary; the agent willed a prisoner into position and froze them there. Often a terrorizing thought was placed in the subject's mind, to torture and torment until the agent was ready to question the subject.

For this subject, Swartz had allowed a tiny bit of the terror stored inside Tan's virus shell. The memory worked very well, he observed. The subject's eyes bulged, as did a vein across its forehead. Through its thick beard, a rictus grin could be seen. Its muscles strained against non-existent bonds, desperately tugging and pulling against its own body. Agents were warned during training to monitor their subject's physical condition closely. Broken bones were not uncommon; from time to time a terrified subject would break its own neck or rupture a blood vessel in the brain, resulting in wasted death and no information.

His supper finished, and the tray cleared away by another agent, Swartz inspected the *Sapiens*. Its flesh hung soft and loose from its lanky frame. Clearly prior to its original enslavement, this one had been heavy, probably obese. Fat slaves were of little use to any master, generally found to be slovenly and lazy. On a ship like *Xian,* with a large number of *Sapiens* and limited supplies, fat slaves would be withheld meals until they proved their value. Records indicated this slave had been highly valued by its former masters. He lowered the intensity of the terror memory.

"You will speak when I speak to you," Swartz instructed. "You will answer my questions completely and accurately. You cannot lie; I will know, and you will be punished. You will speak only Imperial Standard. If your answers please me, you will be rewarded. If I am not pleased…" Swartz shrugged.

"Now, let us begin," said the Intelligence Master. "State your name and occupation."

He released its throat muscles. It cleared its throat several times, then rasped, "I-I-I am Doctor Jakub Tomas Junkers. Might I have some water, please?" It tensed and noiselessly screamed as the nightmare returned to his head full force.

"I asked a question. Answer the question, no more," Swartz said. He dialed back the nightmare. "Where were you taken by you original masters?"

"The village of Luenberg of Tautoun Seven, "it replied.

"Very good. Where were you born?"

"New Munich, Germany on Terra," it said.

"Ah, Germany!" Swartz exclaimed. "So you are a descendant of Junkers royalty."

"I was," it replied. "My father disowned me when I was investigated for subversive activity while in University."

Swartz noted the information for further study. "Where did you get your degree, Herr Doktor?"

"I completed my schooling at Vellarius University. I moved to Tautoun Seven thirty cycles ago for its research opportunities."

"Research opportunities," mused Swartz. "I see it fed you well."

It did not answer. Swartz fed him a large dose of the nightmare. It tensed in its imaginary bonds. Swartz could hear the greasy sound of several joints failing. He eased back slightly, then snapped, "The name of the whore who gave birth to you! Give it to me!"

"My mother was no whore...AHHHHHHH!" it screamed as the nightmare filled its head.

"You are a *Sapiens.* In the New Order, you are less than human. Further, you are a slave, property of the Khan. As such, you will answer the questions asked. Do you understand filthy creature? Now, the name!"

"Juliana. Doctor Juliana Marie von Junkers."

"Very good. Now, the name of the pimp who raped her?" asked Swartz.

"D-d-doctor Viktor Rameses von Junkers."

"What was your job on Tautoun Seven?" asked the Intelligence Master.

"I am…I was Chief of Genetics at Saint Joseph's research hospital, affiliated with Saint Joseph's University," the thing responded. "We were working on post birth genetic elective manipulation. I…we were able to alter one's appearance, correct defects and enhance abilities."

"Ah, you were a genetic cosmetologist," smirked Swartz. "Making the rich and powerful more attractive, more desirable. Such a noble cause, Herr Doctor. Tell me, what role did you serve aboard this vessel?"

"I am director of the incubator section, ensuring the proper transition and preparation of the incubators for the propagation of Sudahar and the augmentons," the thing answered. "We have more potential incubators than we need, so I am also responsible for their storage until we need them or until they achieve sexual maturity for conversion."

"Conversion. You mean the mutilation we found in your nursery," Swartz felt his anger rising. He raised the level of the nightmare slowly.

"Master, please!" begged the thing. "It is the only way to reproduce the Sudahar and the augments. The Feloids have no need of our help in reproduction as they are suited to have kits on their own…"

"Feloids? Who are the Feloids?" pressed Swartz.

"The large cats. They are also hybrids the Sudahar combined with feral predators and Terran DNA. They consider themselves perfect in every way. Since Clementina and the Sudahar have altered them, they refused to allow any of my researchers to touch their DNA in any fashion," said the trembling prisoner. "Be wary of them, Master. They are cunning, powerful, brilliant predators. The Sudahar use them as warriors, scouts, and to keep the Corporation in order."

"We have seen no evidence of your Sudahar on *Xian*," Swartz again ramped up the nightmare. "What evidence do you have of their existence?"

"Master, please!" pleaded the thing on his wall. "The Shurkorov herself left the fleet weeks ago to return to the Home World. I was told the Sudahar Council of the Nine were in their meeting chamber when the Imperial fleet attacked. After the attack, an augmenton came to the nursery with our Feloid master. We were ordered to prepare and inseminate nine incubators with Sudahar zygotes and to accelerate their growth. I assume the Council has been incapacitated or destroyed."

"Where are these incubators now?"

"After I completed the insemination, the incubators were loaded on a trio of swift frigates." Junkers replied. "This was three days after the battle. I was told they were able to recover the council's meditation stones."

Swartz recalled the circular hole amidships on the *Xian*. If the ship survived, he wanted to explore the chamber himself.

"What of the male prisoners?" asked Swartz. "What is their role on this ship?"

"The males?" snorted Junkers. "Those of value to the Corporation, such as myself, were enslaved and allowed to serve. The rest are feed for the Feloids."

Swartz pondered the informant's information for a few minutes. He released it from the nightmares, securing them safely in his virus shell. It hung its head and breathed raggedly.

The things head snapped up suddenly, rigidly. "Now, Doctor," sneered Swartz. "I shall see if you are telling me the truth. Since you are property of the Empire, you have certain rights. I am suspending those rights, as you admitted to participating in subversive activities and performing unapproved medical experiments involving alien species not yet classified by the Empire. I pray for your sake that you were speaking only truth."

Swartz extended his mental probe deep into the mind of the slave, ripping and shredding through it as an excited child opening a great gift. Nothing was left unexposed, not Junkers learning to take his first steps, his first kiss or the confrontation with his father. The anxiousness of young Viktor's doctor's boards at university, the joy Junkers felt when he was awarded his doctorship, the pain of losing his wife when the Sudahar invaded Tautoun Seven.

The obscenities and perversions he committed on the females on this very ship as physician in charge, the liberties he took with the young girls before storing them for future conversion, all flowed through the former doctor's mind. Swartz saw it all. *How fortunate for him he didn't lie to me, he* thought. There was no more information to take. He knew all he needed to know.

"Salinas!" he mind-called. The young girl who had brought him his supper peered in the door. **"I have something here for you to practice on,"** he told her. **"I want you to spend two hours on physical restraint and manipulation. You will practice terror and mind manipulation. See how many bones you can convince it to break, how many joints you can tear.**

When you have finished your two-hour practice, you may kill it."

"Thank you, Master!"

Chapter 17

Thirty hours later

On the very short list of things Katy O'Hare missed about Glanearagh, was the sound of an evening rainfall on the tin roof of her home. It was noisy, but she would listen to the rain clatter against the sheets of tin for hours. She would snuggle deeper into her bed, pulling a quilt over her and leaving only her nose and mouth exposed, savoring the fresh air wafting through her open window. The stink of the factories and the rot from the fishmongers would be washed away; the bouquet of cleaned cobblestones and what little greenery the industrial city possessed would lull her into dreams of the fine, rolling green hills far from Glanearagh she had read about and never seen.

It was a shortcoming for living in space. Katy tried to remember the last time she had sat and listened to a rainfall. Perhaps that wonderful leave she and Andre had shared on Vespa. The heavily forested planet was like nothing she had ever seen: green, wild and fresh. It was difficult to believe that Terra had settled that world. The rain came in the evenings; she and Andre sat on the veranda of their cottage and just watched and listened to the rain for hours, then entered the cabin and made love.

Katy poured another two fingers of Glivenich. It wasn't the second or the third. Hell, she couldn't remember how many she had today. She had drained her flask twice and had a few at lunch as well. She raised the glass as the door chimed, calling, "Enter."

Doctor Ho-Bar strode into her quarters, a musty, burlap covered bottle in his hand. "Here, try this," he snarled. "It'll fuck you up quicker."

"Yeah?" asked Katy. "What about the strychnine?"

"Like that matters?" he answered. "You are killing yourself, anyway. What does it matter quick or slow? At least this way you put us all out of your misery quicker."

"Yeah, yeah. Are you here to lecture me again?" she grumbled.

"No, I am done with the lectures," her friend said. "You're bound and determined to kill yourself. Cut to the chase and do it." He pushed the bottle closer to her.

Katy grabbed the bottle. "Maybe I will," she threatened. "That would make you happy, right? Almighty Doctor Ho-Bar cures another dying patient with his special brand of medicine."

"As opposed to poor, poor Katy O'Hare, martyr of the Fleet," he responded. "Drinking herself to death over her obsession of a single derelict. What ever happened to Commodore Katy O'Hare? That was a woman this fleet had respect for."

"Obsession? Obsession!" she shrieked. "Have you been over there? Have you seen what happened on that cursed ship? How could you see that and not drink? And I have the duty to recover that damned ship."

Ho-Bar pointed a fat finger in her face. "You have a duty to this whole fleet," he said. "Your job is the recovery of all the survivors of this battle. Your job is the salvage of the remains of this battle. Your job is the whole of this system, not just one, single horrific event in an entire solar system of horror."

He slammed his holo on the table. Face after dead face flashed from the cube. "Here's a sample of that horror, Commodore," he seethed. "Imperial officers and ratings who fought and died in this battle. Please, choose for me, which is more horrid, which is more inhumane. Show me the one that means more than the rest. Which of these images should keep me awake tonight? To whom should I drink this whole bottle, so I can sleep tonight?"

She swept the holo from her table and buried her face in her hands, body trembling as suppressed tears flowed freely. Clenched fists slammed the table. "Damn you," she hissed. "Damn you to hell. Who are you to tell me what my job is? I've done nothing but my duty since I escaped that hell-hole back on Terra. The one time, the only time I allow myself to feel...this..."

Ho-Bar replaced the holo on the table. The image showed two young women, girls really, lying side by side in a cubicle. "These two," he said. "My scans show they're sisters. Twins. They've been pumped full of growth hormones. You can't tell, they're only five standard years old. The bastards have accelerated their ages to around twelve or thirteen. Apparently, we found them in time; the slaves were preparing them for their conversion surgery." He stared at the image for a long minute. "These two are the ones who will keep me awake tonight.

"We're all suffering from this, Katy. Everyone who's gone on board that accursed ship is having nightmares from what they've seen, save the engineers working the reactor issue. And they are having nightmares of their own. We need you, Commodore. We need you on the bridge of *Mary Kane* directing this salvage. *Lydia Rae* is rigging the second debris raft now; he'll be ready to depart within twelve hours. The derelict cruiser is rigged for tow; *Taiho* is awaiting permission to depart…"

"Enough!" Katy's fist pounded the com and demanded, "Bridge, Duty Officer!"

"Bridge aye," came the reply. "How can I help you, Commodore?"

"Signals, I want Captain Oooms onboard *Taiho.*" She took a moment to wipe a wet towel over her face and a quick brush of her hair. Ho-Bar settled into a chair, sipping from his bottle. Katy had just alighted back into her chair when a polite chime sounded. The holo of Oooomamoo formed.

In their natural state, the Oooomamoo were formless, shapeless with neither skin or internal organs. Their color ranged from a pale yellow to brilliant red. There seemed no rhyme or reason to the coloration. Katy had sat in a meeting with Oooomamoo and watched them shift colors from one end of their spectrum to the other. When the Empire first came to their world, Zartan Seven (the Empire's name. The Oooomamoo's name for their home was "here,") the residents were amused at the solid forms. Imperial social order entertained them as well. In the Oooomamoo society, each member could co-join with another, then either separate or remerge as a new being.

Imperial technology fascinated the Oooomamoo. While they had created simple tools, the sophistication of the Empire's science drew the Oooomamoo's like a moth to flame. They had science of their own, but it paled in comparison to what these strange creatures from the sky brought. When offered the choice by Imperial diplomats to join the Empire, the Oooomamoo unanimously accepted. They immersed themselves in every aspect of the Empire, flooding schools in every discipline. Hundreds volunteered, as soon as the treaties were signed, for military and civil service.

Finding their formlessness too unsettling to Terrans, the Oooomamoo practiced for years to form themselves into bipeds. They eliminated what they found unnecessary, so there were no fingers or faces, ears or internal organs. There formed rudimentary air bladders and voice boxes to speak.

Captain Oooms of the Taiho was a brilliant yellow this evening, contrasting with its dark green Salvage Corps uniform. A tiny slit at its "neck" fluttered. Oooomamoo mimicked voices they found pleasing, and the Captain's was a raspy whisper.

"Commodore, this one is honored to communicate with you." The voice was a file across brittle plastic. "I understood you have been ill? This one is hoping you are now well."

"Thank you, Captain. I am feeling much better," she said. "I understand *Taiho* is now ready to deliver the salvage cruiser to the scrapping facility at Altamonte?"

"Yes, ma'am, *Taiho* stands by to do his duty," rasped Captain Oooms. "I am waiting for my order."

"Deliver the hulk directly to the scrapyard," ordered Katy. "Instruct the Yardmaster I want the engines removed immediately, to prevent a repeat of its theft. He will have a resupply sled with tow line and engine pods. I need you back within a week."

"Ma'am, it is a six-day journey from here to Altamonte alone," pointed out the yellow featureless face. "I cannot see a way to eliminate five days."

"Yes. Still, I expect you back in one week, Captain," Katy said. "I will contact the Yardmaster personally; I want the sled connected to *Taiho* at record pace. You will be back here in seven days."

"Physics say this is an impossible task," said Captain Oooms. "Therefore, *Taiho* shall find a way to make it happen. Its holo stood and bowed. "With your permission, Commodore?"

"Dismissed," Katy said. "Bridge, Duty Officer, this is the Commodore. Notify Commander Bosley I want a full staff meeting in *Mary Kane's* engineering at 7 A.M. local. All captains and salvage engineers. I want complete reports on the two remaining warships and *Xian*. I want answers as to when we will be able to send them along to the Altamonte scrapyard. Inform the space jack managers I want to see a complete list of every member of this fleet who is space jack qualified and a revised schedule of operations. Tell them to start with my name. I qualified as a space jack when I was an ensign, so you can schedule me to work in twelve hours."

Ho-Bar raised a medical scanner and frowned. "Tell them to schedule her in thirty hours, Lieutenant," he said. "Her electrolytes are low, and she needs to rehydrate."

"Twenty-four hours," Katy decreed and glared at him. "Not a minute more. Agreed?"

"Agreed. But I have your condition recorded, Commodore," he answered. "Food, fluids and rest. No alcohol or stims. I will check before you suit up. If I detect any alcohol, I will suspend your rating. You will be forced to go through a complete physical and recertification. Understood?"

"Agreed. I suggest you go prepare your report, Doctor," ordered Katy. "I will see you at seven A.M." Ho-Bar reached for his bottle. Katy grabbed and held it out of his reach. "No, I may need this later," she said.

Katy and Andre walked hand in hand along the lavender sanded beach. Overhead, the twin moons cast a soft glow, the millions of stars around them watched the lovers stroll on the tideline, gentle waves swirling around their naked feet. The hem of Katy's skirt was soaked; she didn't care. Soon enough, back in their hotel room or perhaps here on the mauve sands, she'd drop the skirt slowly for Andre and lay back to make love.

As though reading her mind, he took her in his arms and nibbled on her neck. "Oh God, Andre," she moaned. He always knew just where to touch her. He sucked gently on her ear lobe, then whispered into her ear, "Commodore O'Hare?"

She snorted, slapping him playfully on his cheek. "Come, my love, none of that," she murmured. She moaned softly as he nibbled her neck and whispered again, more insistently.

"Commodore O'Hare!"

She furrowed her brow and opened her eyes. The moonlight, the sand, Andre…all gone. A moment later she recognized her cabin on the *Mary Kane*. "This is O'Hare," she rasped.

"Commodore O'Hare, this is Engineer Diezac," she recognized the voice now. "Ma'am, I need to speak with you, immediately!"

"Holo," she snapped. In a lower voice she said, "Computer, display O'Hare avatar." Her hair was a mess and she was wearing her sleeping gown. On Diezac's holo emitter, he would see Katy in her uniform, her hair perfect.

Dan Diezac's holo image came into resolution in his work coveralls, impeccable as always. Katy wondered momentarily if the immaculate engineer utilized an avatar as she did to maintain his flawless appearance. "I have wonderful news, Commodore," he said immediately. "We have come up with a way to save the *Xian*. Radford and I were discussing it for the last shift and a half. We've been following the handbook for ejecting the burning reactors. Disconnect the plumbing, pull the mounts and use small drive units away from the ship. It's working fine, but taking too long. We only have sixty hours left and five reactors to eject. One at a time, we won't make it.

"Radford and I agree to cable the remaining reactors together, leave the plumbing joined together, only adding some flex joints here and there. We'll loosen the hardware connecting the reactors to the ship, but we'll also cut the structure so if the bolts don't release, then the framework will give way, freeing the reactors. Finally, we'll pack the biggest motors we can to the first two reactors and use them to rip the other three out."

"It sounds dangerous," Katy responded. "Will it work?"

"It is dangerous," conceded Diezac. "The sudden stress could rip open any one of the reactors, causing a cascade failure. Any one segment could fail to separate. The hull could fail throughout the aft end and rip the ship apart. The only other option is to continue releasing the reactors one at a time and pray we have the time to release the last three. Then there is the issue of control.

"Once we start this zipper method, that's what Hembree calls it, someone has to operate the power plants manually from onboard the reactor. The amount of radiation precludes operating the power plants remotely by radio signal or direct cable hookup. Someone will have to ride the first reactor out of the ship and into space."

"That much radiation will kill whoever volunteers," Katy said. "I forbid you or Hembree from volunteering."

"We understand," said Diezac. "We already have someone who has volunteered. Radford and I agree he is the most qualified."

"Who?"

"Lieutenant Commander Damari Russell."

"Isn't he the one who found the women?" she asked.

"Yes. That is part of the reason he says he has volunteered," explained the Engineer. "He is eminently qualified for the job, if I had to choose, his would be the first name I'd think of. Also," his voice lowered, "Since he made his discovery, he's been in rough shape. He hasn't slept or eaten. He says every time he closes his eyes, he sees that poor woman. I sent him to see Special Agent Tuhnka to see if she could offer him any relief. He returned in even worse shape, although the Special Agent declared him fit for duty."

"I hate the thought of losing such a fine young engineer and abhor the thought of using him this way," Katy sighed. "Is there no other way? Anyone as qualified who would be a better substitute?"

"No, Ma'am," he answered. "I wish there were, but this is our best chance of saving those poor souls."

"All right, I agree," she said. "Have the presentation prepared for this morning's briefing. I assume you will be there?"

"By holo, Ma'am," he said. "We are all busy here setting this up. We haven't a second to lose if we are going to make this work."

"Very well. I expect to see your report in…" she looked at the clock and groaned. It was already five A.M. "Two hours, Dan."

"Understood. Diezac out." The holo deresolved.

Katy flopped back in bed and pulled the pillow over her head. Seconds later, a chime sounded and the tannoy announced, "It is five a.m. This is your wake-up call. It is five a.m. This is your wake-up call..." She sent an evil thought to the creator of the alarm clock, then set about her day. As Commodore, she had a private shower and bath. Icy water awakened her, hot relaxed and loosened her body for the day. While soaping herself, she thought of Andre again, the feel of his strong hands on her body. But Andre was gone, dead for years. Never again would she see him, save in her dreams.

She finished and dressed for her day, regulation slacks and blouse. When reaching for her sweater, Katy hesitated. The sweater was warm, comfortable, a pleasant reminder of a happier time in her life, when she was more carefree, and the future stretched out before her seemingly infinite.

Until this mission, that was precisely how she felt, even after all these years. Engineer Russell was haunted by the remains of the woman he had seen. Diezac and Hembree were working themselves beyond exhaustion trying to save this nightmare ship, save the doomed souls left behind. Katy O'Hare was facing her own demons, having seen both the colonists and the remains of the enemy who had done this. Space was no longer a refuge for her. It had become a terrifying hallucination, a vision of the most despicable thing a life form could impose on another. She now had no delusions that space was a safe vocation. Indeed, her career as a naval officer had reinforced the dangers of this chosen career.

The red headed augmentons killing her soldiers. The mysterious and unseen Sudahar in charge of the whole operation, from the mutilation of the females to the giant cats eating the males.

She ran her hand along the sleeve's cable stitched wool, then reached for her Naval Officer jacket.

The fit was snug, snugger than Katy would want to admit. As she prepared to leave her stateroom for breakfast, she spied the silver flask. There was no room for it in her uniform. *Just a nip then. Just a wee drap to clean the sleep from my mouth and steady my nerves.* She started to reach for her old friend when she spied the burlap covered bottle Ho-Bar left the night before.

Commodore O'Hare straightened her jacket and marched resolutely out the door.

Chapter 18

Max didn't know his last name. Not that it mattered or that he really cared. He'd been raised on Pym, an industrial world out on the Rim, just past the Imperial border. Pym boasted a massive junkyard in orbit, where obsolete and stolen ships were stored. The yardmaster regularly cleared up space (and added to his bank account) by selling the ships to the foundries on the planet, where they would be melted down or recycled for usable materials for sale to manufacturing worlds. Max's father had died at a foundry; with no real government to regulate the planet, accidents were frequent, and workers died by the thousands.

After his father died, Max's mother would go out into the streets at night. She was a handsome woman and earned a good enough living for herself and her ten-year-old son. Until the night she went out and was never seen again.

Hard-faced men threw the boy out of the family apartment and squatted in it for themselves. Max, a big child for ten, soon hooked up with a local youth gang that ran the streets. As he grew into a teen, he became well known for his fast fists and ill-temper. Grown men would sooner cross the street than confront the short-fused boy.

At sixteen, the orphan screwed up. Badly. He was in a bar, pouring down a few. (That he was under-aged never came up. Few bartender and fewer bouncers would cross "Angry Max.") A loudmouthed dandy in an expensive suit and surrounded by three of his best friends chided and pushed Max too far. In the end, the three friends were in various states of permanent disfigurement and the dandy boy had his neck splintered, his head turned nearly completely around.

When he sobered up in the jailhouse, Max began the course his life would take for the next ten years. He performed an unmentionable sexual act for a jailer, who conveniently allowed the teen to escape. Max stowed away on a small freighter, leaving Pym forever. The crew caught him and the captain, rather than space the boy, put him to work. Max found he enjoyed being an ordinary spaceman. He stuck around that freighter for several months before imbibing too much on an outpost and missing the ship when it left.

No matter. He survived for two months the way he had back on Pym, strong arm robbery with the occasional honest day's work. When the cops got too close, he'd hop over to the spaceport and take a job, any job, on a ship leaving the system, avoiding Imperial planets as best he could. Someone had given him a copy of the Laws of Angkor Khan, the code which defined Imperial Law. Max tried to read it, but since he had dropped out of school after his mother disappeared and reading was for spoofs anyway, he could barely make heads or tails of the thick book. So he threw the book away and promised himself to avoid the Empire as much as possible.

Inevitably, he found himself on an Imperial outpost near the Rim. He heard there was a good time to be found on the planet, so he used his best forged identification to try and enter. It failed the scan and he was detained in a small, white room, seated on an uncomfortable chair, his hands cuffed to a bar on the tabletop. After an hour, a tall middle-aged woman in a black uniform entered. She regarded him as one would an insect or a gatnek grub. "Well, weren't you a hard case!" Her voice was unpleasantly deep with a snooty spoofs accent. She settled into the other chair and stared. "Your name is Max Swang. Our records show you have an interesting history. Larceny, assault, rape, murder…" her voice lilted up when she said murder. "Fortunately for you, these crimes all occurred outside Imperial space and we are disinclined to prosecute you for crimes not occurring inside our borders.

"However, this also means you are not a citizen and protected by the Laws of the Individual. I am Imperial Intelligence and I am going to deep scan you to verify you have not committed any crimes in our space." Max felt icy tendrils thrust into his scalp and squeeze his brain. He tried to scream, but his lungs wouldn't fill with air. His chest was wrapped in a tight iron band, refusing to allow him one, single breath. He had nearly drowned once, diving in a deep tourist fountain to steal coins. Chocking on a viscous fluid, panic at not knowing where to turn, the inability to simply breathe.

Then it was over. The agent said, "Fortunate, for you anyway. I'm sure your victims would disagree. You are banned from Imperial space. Should you attempt to enter our space you will be arrested, marked and deported. Should you prove to be persistent, then it will be assumed you wish to enter our justice system. Be assured, you will not have a long or productive life should you come to our attention again. If I were you, I would try my utmost to stay out of the Empire."

They put him on an outgoing freighter and Max was no dummy. He studiously avoided Imperial ships and worlds from that day forward. The telepath in the black uniform had done something no one had ever succeeded in doing. Max had become terrified.

Max eventually screwed up again eight years later. Sauer Nine was a mid-tech world with a wild party reputation. He decided he wanted to see for himself if the reputation was deserved or not. Coin jingled in his pocket as he wandered out into port town.

Hours later, Max came to the conclusion the reputation was indeed well deserved. He located some stims, ate a magnificent supper and commenced to some hard-core drinking and gambling. He put all his skills to use in the card games and did well until the house dicks discovered his cheating and threw him out. Whistling tunelessly, he'd amble to the next card house and rack up more winnings until they caught on.

Somewhere between the fourth and fifth card house, he saw her. Pretty little thing wearing the gauzy pantaloons and vest Sauer Nine's women wore. She was walking hurriedly, her head low. The animal lust in Max awoke. He let out a low growl and went into his hunt mode. Max slid one block over, then ran two blocks up. Concealing himself in an alley, he waited until she began to pass. A muffled shriek went unheard in the cacophony of reveling in this part of town, his hands over her mouth and smooth, soft midriff.

Behind an overflowing trashbin would do. He fell on top of her, ripping the pantaloons open, then pulling his own trousers down.

She cried and struggled. He liked that, when they tried to fight him off. He never met a woman who could stand up to him. This one was like all the others, eventually submitting to his strength. When he finished, he barely noticed she had stopped struggling. Not even whimpering like they always did. Oh well, no matter. Max pulled up his pants and made his way back to his hotel. A good night's sleep, then he'd leave this little paradise. Nice enough place; he'd make sure he came back some other time.

The next morning was life changing for Max. He had slept well, dressed and packed. Over a final cup of breakfast coffee, the cops showed up. They didn't act like cops on any of the other worlds he had been arrested. Rather than politely walking over to him and asking his name, they pointed their weapons at him and fired. Max toppled from his chair, conscious but stunned, easy prey for the restraint web that dragged him away.

Max's free barrister provided him with bad news on top of bad news. The girl he had raped was under aged. Worse, she died of the rape's injuries. If that wasn't bad enough, the last news staggered him.

It hadn't been announced yet, of course, otherwise Max would have avoided Sauer Nine. Its government was tired of the world's lawless regions; even more frightened of the pirates and nearby worlds who had designs on their resources. So the government had accepted the invitation of the mighty Terran Empire to become a client world, live under Imperial protection, follow Imperial law. It would be the first step to joining the Empire and the benefits that membership would provide.

Max would not receive any of those benefits.

The evening before his trial, he was to be interviewed by an Imperial Intelligence agent. Secured to a table in a conference room as he had years before when he first encountered Imperial Intelligence, he kept a brave front, but inside was terrified. The thought of another mind scan made his gut twist. Then, through the door sauntered a short Asian woman, a girl really, wearing the black uniform he remembered. In the opposite chair, she sat and smiled. At the smile, Max wet himself.

"Well, we won't be needing these." The voice was in his head! The manacles at his hands and feet fell away. He tried to lunge but couldn't. Her probing emerald eyes captivated him, drew him in and held him in place.

"Stand, strip, then stand with your back one inch away from the wall, arms raised to shoulder height, fingers extended, palms down."

Max wanted to disobey the orders, struggled in his mind: *NO! STOP! I will not do this! You can't make me!* His body rose from the chair and complied with her instruction.

"Very good. Stop breathing and listen. I am Special Agent Tan of Imperial Intelligence. Raise the fingers of your right hand by the first joint until I say stop.

Seemingly by their own will, the fingers of his right hand raised. There was resistance as the ligaments and bones reached a maximum angle, but the muscles in his hand continued to pull them back. He tried to screech as a greasy crunch came from his hand.

"Stop. You may breathe now."

He gasped and wailed at the pain, trying first to close his hand, then trying urgently to grab his hand with the other. There must have been unseen restraints; he couldn't move his right arm. Nor could he writhe in pain.

"Very good. Right kneecap now."

The muscles in his right leg moved, independent, twisting and pulling his kneecap to the side and inverting it.

"Spine."

Why couldn't he faint? He screamed as his back muscles pulled his vertebrae this way and that, contorting his back, moving his hips sideways, his shoulders separating, the left forced up like a hump, the right shoved to dovetail his ribs.

"You will stop screaming now and listen. You have been charged with rape of an underage child and murder caused by this rape. Under the Laws of my Grandfather and the Codes of the Khalkha from which those codes arose, your punishment will be public castration followed by impalement. That means we shove the impalement spear up your ass until it comes out your skull. You'll die, but a skilled executioner will make sure you live for five, maybe six days before you slowly bleed out. I have

contacted our Ministry of Justice; our very finest executioner is prepared to travel here for your punishment.

But the Empress is also quite merciful and understanding. She believes, as do I, given the right circumstances you might be rehabilitated into a useful, productive member of society. You will be required to be kept under constant surveillance and will serve me as a bound and indentured servant until I am convinced this nasty disease of civil disobedience and anti-social behavior is eradicated from you."

So, what is your answer to be, Max Swang? Is it to be castration and impalement or do you surrender to me for rehabilitation?"

"Lady, please, whatever you want," groaned Max. "Please, just make it stop hurting."

His ruined body collapsed to the floor. Twisted joints, broken bones and raw nerves demanded his attention.

"Oh, quit your whining. I swear, you *Homo Sapiens* have such a low tolerance for a little pain. Now, up, up, up. I have your paperwork to finish and you need to exercise your new body. Oh, shoot, one last thing.

Max felt and heard the familiar greasy creak as his jaw dislocated on the right side and hung loosely. A cold metal finger stirred in his brain.

"There. Now I don't have to listen to any more of your complaining."

Max lay on the pile of rags in a cargo hold of the *Mary Kane*. When Tan had first reported aboard, she explained the ruined human was a pet project of sorts, a rehabilitation Intelligence was trying on a particular brand of criminal. This one, sadly, had been rescued from a shipwreck, was the crew's information. She'd worked with him for five years and this was as good as he was going to get, poor soul.

Max was treated well aboard *Mary Kane,* somewhat of a cross between a mascot and a pet. He was given simple cleanup jobs; usually unpleasant ones other crewmen were assigned but didn't want to do. A pleasant side effect was that *Mary Kane* had the cleanest heads in the fleet.

Unknown to the crew, when Tan had a mission that needed speed, strength and stealth, she would restore Max to his previous condition and set him on his way. Always afterwards, he returned to her to be mutilated and resume his role aboard *Mary Kane.* It took skillful manipulation of the crew's mind when she sent him out on a task, but after the first three, the crew was generally accepting of her mental manipulations.

On this day, Max lay on his pile of rags, weeping silently. Even after five years, his body ached constantly. Before and after missions were the worse as his body would contort into whatever form Tan wished. He prayed to whatever gods he had heard about in his past to end his suffering. Hourly, he wished he had chosen impalement.

"Max, darling, wake up. Stop asking yourself if you would have been better off dying. Look how much good you have done for the Empire! You should be proud to bear a little pain for the glory of the Khan! Now, up, up, up. I have one final mission for you."

Did she say final mission? Max's heart skipped a beat. He struggled to his feet and shuffled to Mistress Tan's quarters.

Chapter 19

The fleet retreated to a safe distance from *Xian*. In ten minutes, his fate would be known. Either the five burning reactors would be yanked free from the ship or a chain reaction would be the end of the *Xian*.

On the bridge of the *Mary Kane*, Katy had assumed her customary position slightly off center of the main display. The burning section of *Xian* dominated the main holo. In a corner of the display, Damari Russell was tucked away in a hastily rigged command pod connected to the forward reactor in the sequence. He was already a dead man, his skin blistered and peeling. The ropes of dreadlocks under his watch cap were shedding from the intense radiation. His scratchy voice could be barely made out in the flood of voices aboard *Mary Kane* and the rest of the ships involved in the operation.

The pod had been wrapped in every manner of shield and insulating blanket, but those precautions had little effect against the runaway reactors. Russell himself had shunned wearing a radiation suit. "It's gonna give me, what, five more minutes?" he said. "Nah, I'll leave it outside the pod with my tenders. No sense to leaving it wrapped around my dead-assed body."

A soft chime sounded in her earpiece. "Commodore, *Lydia Rae* calling," announced the comm officer. "He is requesting permission to depart with the second debris raft." Katy tapped a control; a third small holo appeared, a bulky bald man. Captain Chuck Graham was already a flag officer when Katy was an ensign. She was surprised and pleased to see him volunteer to join her flotilla years ago when she first commanded the salvage fleet. Captain Graham was nearly one hundred years old and showed few signs of slowing up and none of retiring.

He spoke first. "*Mary Kane,* this is *Lydia Rae* calling. Request permission to detach from the fleet to deliver my scrap haul."

"*Lydia Rae, Mary Kane,*" responded Katy. "Permission granted. Good to see you again, Captain Graham. May the ancients watch over your mission. We'll see you back in ten days."

Graham said, "That boy driving your *Xian* operation. Brave lad. A credit to the service." He snapped a sharp salute. "Ten days, Commodore." The holo snapped out.

Katy visualized the departure of *Lydia Rae.* The tachyon emitters extending from the front of the tug like whiskers, blue light of tachyons firing to a point forward of the ship, coalescing and opening space just far enough to accept the tug and the debris sled, then closing without a trace.

The chatter stopped as Diezac announced, "Five minutes." Everyone, save Katy and the boyish engineer, focused on their instruments. Russell said, "*Xian* acknowledges, five minutes." He paused, "Hey, Dan."

"Yeah, Damari?"

"Not what we expected, huh?"

"Nope."

"Better, though. This way I mean," Damari said. Then, hesitantly, "Hey, Dan?"

"Yes?"

"You talk to my mom, O.K.?" Damari said. "You tell her... You tell her I volunteered, right? Tell her this was the best way, the right thing to do. I'm here because I want to be."

"Yeah, sure, Damari, I'll tell her," Diezac said. "I'll make sure she understands. Is that a fluctuation on power unit two?"

"Yeah, damnit. Hold on. There we go," Damari replied. His voice sounded scratchier. "Two minutes. Powering up all propulsion units. Have Captain Cavner blow the skin plates now."

"Roger."

Seconds later, orange tracers raced across the aft hull of the *Xian,* around the burning reactors. Hull plates fluttered away like chips falling from the woodsman's axe.

"One minute."

"Hey, Dan, one last thing," announced Damari. "You make damn sure they spell my name right when they dump me in the Red Queen's Necropolis. It's Russell with two s's and two l's."

"Got it. Ten seconds."

"All right. Powering up," said Damari. "Hit the releases in three... two...one...release."

A bulge formed at the forward end of the burning plasma. It swelled and rose from the *Xian,* solidifying into the seventy-foot diameter, one hundred foot burning reactor, the plasma flame illuminating the space around it in its white glow. The four power plants paled in blue flame by comparison. Damari Russell's control pod was obscured by the colorful plume of the burning plasma as entrails of plumbing followed the reactor along with the tow lines connecting to reactor two. Seconds later, an identical second cylinder lifted free. Ten-foot engine pods strapped to the reactors blazed blue flame, lifting them free of the ship. "Damari, if you can hear me, throttle up to one hundred five percent," Dan called in the clear. The blue flames lengthened, and the first two reactors jumped to one side as the tow lines grew taught. Everyone held their breath as the third, then the fourth reactors pulled free.

The lines tightened on the fifth reactor. The line of reactors jerked and swayed, the last reactor refusing to break free. *Xian* began to wobble as the fiery line convulsed, flailing to pull the reluctant bomb free of the ship. Suddenly, the engines on the first two pods fired in sequence, stopping the wild gyration, arcing the entire string that pivoted around *Xian's* stern. The stuck reactor finally ripped free, tearing a hundred-foot hole in the stern. *Xian* wobbled just a moment more and then resumed its stately orbit.

The string of glowing reactors, free of the *Xian,* reacted to the immutable laws of motion, pin-wheeling away at sickening speed, flinging debris and fire. The troublesome fifth reactor tore away from the string, spinning wildly before exploding in nuclear fire. The force of the explosion added an angular wobble to the spin of the reactors as the constellation of fire rapidly tumbled away.

"Comm, fleet wide," ordered Commodore O'Hare. When the officer nodded, Kate ordered, "Fleet, attention! Salute!"

Max restrained himself from dancing as he strolled down the passageway of *Tranquility*. To be whole again, free of the wretched, twisted body his mistress kept him in when he wasn't performing a mission. Tonight's, she had told him, would be his last. He couldn't wait to get free of the Imperials, their condescending looks and comments when he was not whole. To be free of their *glarpshite* rules and laws.

To be free of his mistress.

What would he do first? He had dreamed for years of his soon to be newfound freedom. He would get stimmed up, then rip roaring drunk. His dexterity was a little off, so no cardsharping for a while. And a piece of ass. Young, pretty and totally obedient to his wishes. In his whole condition, no woman he chose would stand a chance against his deprivation. And he was hungry. Very, very hungry.

An ache formed in his head, just behind his eyes. His mind was drifting from the mission. The ache was her reminder to focus. He stood outside the door, fingering the tiny box in his pocket. It was a neutralizer, she had told him, focused for his target's brain specifically. He pressed the switch on the side, hoping his mistress wasn't toying with him. If a telepath like his mistress could do this to him, what could a powerful telepath like his target do?

Max entered the Tuhnka's room where the light was low. Terrans, even advanced telepaths, needed the darkness to maintain their circadian rhythm. The only illumination was a small lamp near the door and from the bathroom. He moved to her bed and gasped. The illumination was enough to reveal Tuhnka to his ravenous eyes. The woman lay on her back, one leg crossing the other, her thighs open. She was wearing white panties and a short shirt, exposing her flat stomach and pulled tightly over full, firm breasts. Arms flung wide, head tipped back, she snored softly. Her golden hair was a halo. His beast stirred.

Intense pain returned behind his eyes. Tan had warned him Tuhnka was strikingly beautiful and would distract him with her body. This painful reminder threatened to burn a hole through his mind. He fumbled in his pocket, pulled out the syringe and plunged it quickly into the artery in the sleeping woman's neck, pressed the plunger dispensing the drug. Her eyes snapped open, opal fire glaring, her mouth moving to speak just as the toxin took effect. Tuhnka's body locked rigid, only her breasts heaving as she struggled to breathe. He accepted the pain in his head for the moment it took him to reach down and rub the inside of her thigh.

Tan also warned him the toxin would not last long. He unrolled the standard body bag and wrapped her in it, straightening her legs and placing her arms across her chest. When activated, it clung tightly to a body, leaving only its face exposed. This one was strong, already throwing off some of the effects of the toxin, her body starting to quiver in the tight wrapping. Max covered her face with the flap provided and initiated the grav-null.

At this hour of night, the shadowy passageway was devoid of any wandering crewman. He took the most direct route to a waiting Tan. The airlock door was open, Tan smirking as he pulled her sister into the chamber and deactivated the nulls. Tuhnka was no longer rigid; the toxins allowing her body its usual pliability. They positioned her, seated, against a bulkhead.

Tan opened the flap. **"Ah, Sister, I cannot tell you how long I've waited to have you just where you are right now,"** she gloated.

"Indeed, Sister?" responded Tuhnka. **"You know this will only make your death that much slower, more painful when I kill you. Release me now and perhaps I will show you some small mercy."**

"Kill me? Ha! Father has not released you from his order; you don't have his permission to kill me. I, on the other hand, have no such restriction," Tan said. **"Further, I fully intend to make your death as horrid and painful as possible. Allow me to demonstrate."**

Tan entered Tuhnka's mind and found the virus bomb. **"Imagine, Father personally vouched for this when he placed it in your mind. Do you feel even the slightest amount of outrage and betrayal?"** She opened the virus just a bit, allowing the terror of the colonists to flood Tuhnka's mind. Her sister gasped and moaned. **"Isn't this exquisite?"** Tan asked. **"Here, just a bit** more. **Maybe some of my own fury this time."** Tuhnka wailed as her mind was overfilled with Tan's anger mixed with the suffering colonists'.

"Stop, please!" whimpered Tuhnka.

"Begging? And with your voice, like a *Homo Sapiens*? Are you conceding to be an inferior, dear sister?" Tan asked. **"What if I give you more? Will you concede you are inferior?"**

"NO! Never! I am the super…. AHHHHHHHHHHH!" screamed Tuhnka, both from her mind and her voice. Tan had opened the virus fully, exposing her sister to its full effect. For ten eternal minutes Tuhnka screamed and wailed, writhing in the body bag, banging her head against the bulkhead as the suffering of the tens of thousands victims haunted her. Pale, eviscerated bodies, headless souls and stumbling, crawling sub-human remains chased her through the hidden passages in her mind. Above her, around her was Tan, gloating and hurling balls of rage and anger.

Tan closed the valve, leaving Tuhnka a shuddering hulk, weeping piteously. "Please, no more," she begged. "No more. No more." Tan pulled the hood from Tuhnka's head, gripped her by her golden hair, twisting her to face Tan. **"All our lives, we've been raised as *Homo Superior*. Of our eight, you always passed yourself as more superior to the rest of us. You were bigger, stronger, and more beautiful. Father's favorite destined to lead us and produce the next generation of *Homo Superior*. Perhaps even becoming the sa-Khan who would lead us in the war against the *Homo Sapiens*.**

"During my training at the Palace of Giza, I made an astounding discovery. I am a hybrid, the bridge between *Homo Superior* and *Homo Imperious,* the next generation of Terran. I am farther above you in the evolutionary chain than you are of my pet, Max, here. Our Grandfather Noire split our line from the Imperial line more than five hundred years ago to create my unique pattern. The Crown Prince himself has reviewed my DNA and agreed my sequence must be introduced to the Imperial line to create *Homo Imperious.* Imagine, Sister, after five hundred years, the Black line will be re-introduced into the Imperial line, casting out the useless Silver line.

"My Crown Prince will lead the Empire, Sister. Our children will bear my patterns and one-day rule not just the Empire, but the Galaxy as a whole. I will replace father as sa-Khan and the *Homo Imperious* line in Imperial Intelligence will march hand in hand with the Khan as we subdue both the aliens and the *Homo Sapiens.* Oh, how glorious it will be.

"You, dear sister, have no role in the future, save you are the next obstacle in my way. And, do understand, this is entirely personal. If there is any question in your mind, I am totally enjoying watching your humiliation. And your death."

"Max, come remove this infernal device," Tan ordered. He deactivated the body bag, removed it from the quivering woman. Tuhnka wrapped her arms around herself, trying to cover her body from Max's leer. "Does she please you, Max?" Tan asked. He nodded, licking his lips.

"Well, since I agreed this is our last mission together and since you have been an excellent servant and agent, I release you from my service. Tuhnka here is your reward for a job well done. When you are finished with her, you and I shall work on our arrangements for getting you out of the Empire. Enjoy." She opened the virus in Tuhnka's mind a final time and left the airlock.

Tuhnka's screams could barely be heard through the bulkhead. It wasn't entirely the faces of the Damned in her mind. Max had ripped away her clothing and was mauling her. His strong hands attacked her breasts; he licked her face and bit her on the neck and mouth. Tan almost roiled in revulsion as Max dropped his trousers and violated her sister. Almost. She gave him five minutes, then tapped the control for the outer door. The couple, joined in coitus, were sucked into space. This airlock was carefully chosen; it was aimed directly at the Joeanmika Star. It might take weeks, but the bodies would eventually be destroyed as they plunged into the sun.

She hadn't lied to Max, she mused. Technically, they were outside the Empire. Her arrangements just didn't involve him leaving with a spaceship. *I'm sure he appreciated this way far more than the impalement spear*, she thought.

Well, that's done with. Now to deal with my father.

Chapter 20

"Well, lookie here, crew! We got Mopsie coming out to play!" The catcalls came from the depths of *Mary Kane*'s space jack locker room. Katy blushed. Within the small community of space jacks there were few secrets and fewer forbidden topics.

One requirement for all cadets in the Academy was participation in a team sport. Katy had chosen Null-G futboll. She had excelled in anti-gravity training, so trying for the popular game that placed more value on speed, agility and guile was a clever choice. The sprite of a cadet outclassed any player in the domed playfield, moving magically through the open space, handling the ball as though it were an extension of her own body. Her passes were crisp and accurate; she seemingly scored at will. There was talk of her drafting her to play in the next cycle of the Empire Cup. Katy refused, of course. She was focused on her career.

Katy had earned the name "Mopsie" from her head of thick, wild red hair. She kept it tied back in a fat pony tail, but it seemed to have a life of its own as she dashed and darted about in the low gravity. Early in her freshman year, while playing in the traditional match against Imperial Army Academy, a sports commentator broadcasting the match called her the cute nickname. It stuck and spread throughout the sport for her full four years. She only escaped it after graduation when her first assignment was to Euencladius.

The nickname popped up from time to time, but only within the tight community of space jacks.

Doctor Ho-Bar had called her to medical and quickly verified Katy was sober and in shape to work. She raced to the locker room, eager to gear up for the shift. Stripping and powdering her body made the tight-fitting undergarment easier to don. The over garment, a thin, white, full body suit, was studded with sensors and biofeedback actuators to assist the space jack operating the jack unit. Katy found the gossamer garment comfortable, though for a sixty-seven-year-old woman perhaps a tad revealing. Then again, no one in the locker room stared.

She did a few deep knee bends, twisted and flexed. The material clung to her like a second skin, sliding smoothly with her every movement. Excellent.

A dozen attendants awaited next to the six EVA suits. Five were brilliant white, modern units. The sixth was once the brilliant gold of an Imperial Navy space jack. Forty years later, the gold had been sun-bleached to a flat yellow/brown with a dozen black, brown and orange repairs. Fifty colorful patches covered Katy's EVA suit, souvenirs of duty stations and difficult missions.

She settled back into the suit as her technicians connected the forty leads of biofeedback and communications. Chief Corvine, the Lead suit technician onboard *Mary Kane,* personally connected Katy to her suit. As always, he asked, "Sure I can't get you something a little more up to date, Mopsie? Maybe something built in this century?"

Katy smiled as Chief Corvine lowered her helmet. He had polished the gold-plated hood to a brilliant sheen. The shamrock she hand painted forty years before was recently rejuvenated, she noted, gleaming in the bright lights of the preparation room. Once the helmet activated, Katy reviewed the mission while Chief Corvine fitted her gloves and completed the hook-ups.

"Everybody ready?" called Jack Verdine, the team leader. All six space jacks entered the airlock at the aft end of the room, exiting on the bottom side of the *Mary Kane.* Another dozen handlers awaited them, escorting the space jacks to their work frames, the yellow vehicles that each space jack would operate during the mission. The rigs were mounted to a cutter that would ferry the space jacks to their assigned positions.

The space jack required assistance into the cockpit. One handler placed his feet on either side of Katy and pulled the restraint belts tight. Katy gasped as they tightened. Hundreds of methods had been devised over the centuries to secure a space jack to his work frame. Nothing had ever proven to be more secure, simpler than a series of straps with a central quick release. The other handler connected her to the frame: life support, comm, control. She gave Katy a thumbs up and watched as the Commodore ran the rig through its test profile.

The rig was a ten-foot open frame with four fifteen-foot articulated arms. Behind the operator was the power plant and computers. Small thrusters dotted the rig. Each was fueled for a twelve-hour working mission, searching for debris packages gathered together by drones, gathering and directing them to the newest debris raft. Four of the space jacks would find the debris and direct the debris to Katy, who in turn would redirect them to the raft. The sixth, Jack Verdine, supervised the whole mission, helping where needed and making sure his charges were safe.

Katy's attendants slapped her helmet and scurried back into the ship. Moments later, the cutter, its sextet secure, departed *Mary Kane* and maneuvered into space. At her designated point, Katy was released into open space.

The cutter moved away swiftly. Katy turned her white noise generator up, blocking the noises of her suit and the work frame, leaving her with the silence of the comm and her own breathing. For the first time since this mission started, Katy was totally relaxed. She tapped her steering control, allowing the frame to spin slowly, with wonders of the local universe panning around her. No ship, nor any of the space jacks, could be seen. Each had blurred into any of the infinite number of spots of light moving through a vast universe.

Katy was always astounded that, for all its vastness, space was *crowded*. Distant stars and nebulae slowly orbit around her. Far in the distance, she knew the smallest spots of light were galaxies farther away than Terrans could ever travel, each the size of her Milky Way and larger. In her frame, she extended her arms and legs wide, stretching her back while reveling in the cosmic magnificence. The frame matched her every move, extending itself as well, stretching to its limits. Katy groaned with pleasure and said, "Gods, if there are really any Gods out there, thank you for this magnificent view of your universe."

"You're welcome." The voice was in her ear, followed by a chuckle. "Did you forget the hot mike, Mopsie?" called team leader Verdine. Katy reddened, remembering at that moment that the microphone was left hot while they were working. "Got your first inbound, e.t.a... five minutes."

"Roj," Katy answered. The information was displayed on her wide visor. Fifteen feet long, ten wide. One metric ton. The transducer showed its approach was straight forward, no twist, no rotation. No need to drastically change its orbit, just a few degrees. She decided to get fancy, twisting the frame and catching the lump of trash with her right boot and kicking it on its way toward the raft.

"Oooooooo," came the catcalls. "Somebody playing fancy." Katy laughed; they fed her a softball and expected a safe grab and toss. This wasn't her first mission; she needed to show these youngsters she'd been space jackin' before most of them had been borne.

"Next inbound, nine minutes," announced Verdine. "Let's see what you do with this, Mopsie."

The display showed the debris was larger, fifty feet long, ten wide. Twenty tons. Slightly radioactive. An engine pod. It was twisting on two axes. No fancy kicks this time. She opened the frame's arms wide and started its rotation to match the engine pod. More taps on her steering jets, then her tumble matched. The distance narrowed and when it was near enough, Katy grappled the pod. It took several moments to arrest the tumble, start the pod on a new rotation and send it on its way to the debris raft.

More hoots and catcalls, this time tinged with appreciation. It had been a tricky move, Katy knew. A veteran move, not to be tried by a rookie or an older woman who hadn't worked a rig for nearly ten years. *Yeah, well these kids don't know ol' Katy O'Hare.* Verdine called out the next target, fifteen minutes out.

Ten hours later, she acknowledged she really was "old" Katy O'Hare. Even with all the servos and feedback mechanisms, Katy was beginning to wear out. The next piece of wreckage was twenty minutes out. A seventy-foot cube, weighing thirty-six tons. Power core, her readout said. A nice break before a tricky catch and throw. She sipped at her water bulb and sucked down the protein jelly lovingly called "space jack candy". It tasted vile, a cross between rotted socks and stomach acid in the back of your throat, but it contained all the nutrition a space jack would need to survive and energize for a twelve-hour shift. The joke was, it would keep you alive…but leave you wondering if you wanted to be alive.

"Still with us, Mopsie?" The call came from Jordy Rivers, one of her team.

"Yeah Jordy. Just eating some of the liquid death," she replied. "How you grow up to be a big strong space jack on this gloppenshite is beyond me."

The laughter of her five team mates jammed her comm. "You eat a lot before you go out," Jordy suggested. "Then starve your way through shift and eat like a taurswine when you get back. You holding up O. K.?"

"I'll make the end of the shift, but it'll be a shower, dinner and bed when we get back to *Mary Kane,*" she said. "Not necessarily in that order."

That brought another round of tired laughter and jeers. This was what was missing. The camaraderie. Her staff and crew on *Mary Kane* and throughout the fleet had a professional relationship, a command structure with her at the top. Here, amongst space jacks, she was "one of the guys", a part of a crew where there were no salutes, no honors, not high airs. Just the crew and the job they had to do. No secrets, no sacred cows.

Katy looked to the stars again. She could stare at the vista for hours and, indeed, had often done so. Something didn't look right. A thin straight line was forming. It grew, horizontal to her bearing. The dark line showed a fringe of blue!

"Space fold!" she screamed over the comm as the proximity alarms went off in all the crew's headsets.

"Everybody break NOW, HARD!" ordered Verdine. All the space jacks were already accelerating away as more openings appeared in the space around the solar system. It wasn't supposed to happen, beacons in otherspace warned when space jacks were operating in real space. But accidents happened. Or deliberate incursions.

Katy accelerated away, keeping the growing blue fringed line in sight. The trick was to move away as fast as you could, then when the prow of the starship came through, to angle away. Then to keep running until the team leader declared a rally point.

The prow of the ship appeared. A big prow. Now that she could see the ship, Katy selected an angle away at forty-five degrees. The ship kept coming. A warship, certainly. But whose?

A broad, grey and black arrowhead, then further out on each side appear a pair of launch bays. The hull continued out, joining the arrowhead with the launch bays. Katy recognized the ship. An Imperial Command carrier, the behemoths normally accompanied with an entire Battle Fleet. On the belly of the growing beast was the symbol of the Terran Empire, a spread wing hawk grasping a blue and green globe in its talons, a pair of swords crisscrossing through the globe.

Eventually, the colossal star drive appeared. The design hadn't changed in centuries. There was no need. The forward half of the mile-long ship was star shaped with launch and recovery bays at the four side points. He had a barrel shaped midsection containing hundreds of missile batteries and close in weapons. The aft third of the ship was the star drive that propelled the warship across the universe.

His exit closed the slice in the fabric of space. Powerful steering jets stopped the carrier inside its own length. His stern pitched up, pivoting on the prow, twisting to port and stabilizing with the prow pointed directly at Katy. She was staring down the maw of his twin meson rifles mounted in the bow. Faceted mirrors ran from the opening to deep within the ship, the meson generators that fueled the weapons glowed with malevolence. In the mirrors Katy could see herself reflected a thousand times.

"Commodore O'Hare, the is the Imperial Command Carrier *Ashira,* of the First War Fleet, led by the Crown Prince Abdul bin Russolov Khan. He directs you to report aboard immediately."

"*Ashira,* this is Commodore O'Hare. Wilco. I will return to *Mary Kane* to make myself presentable, then shuttle to *Ashira.*"

After a long pause, a peevish voice responded. "Commodore, what part of immediately do you fail to understand?"

"I've been working a ten hours shift as a space jack. I need a shower and a clean uniform before I present myself to the Crown Prince," barked Katy.

"The Crown Prince did not allow you time to dally," came the reply. "I am sure this would be acceptable to those serving on the Rim, but in the Imperial Fleet, when one is told immediately, it means at once. Dock on port side forward landing bay."

Serving in the Imperial Fleet clearly did not improve one's manners, thought Katy. "Very well," she announced. "Proceeding to port-forward docking bay."

As she wheeled her ship around the fleet carrier, she contacted Jack. "Listen, tell the fleet to continue operations. Give me a count, let me know how many ships he brought. I want to know how big the boot on my neck is."

"Wilco, Commodore. Good luck."

Katy swung her pod to the named landing port. Automatics pulled her in and berthed it with similar rigs. Handlers disconnected her from the frame as a Naval Commander in a spotless uniform urged her on. "The Crown Prince is not one to be left waiting," he said. They boarded a trolley which moved swiftly along the length of the ship to the command deck.

Katy struggled not to look surprised when they stopped. A column of Marines in battle armor lined the passageway, their rifles at salute. Katy stiffened and strolled down the column as she would if this were the parade ground at the Academy.

The Command Center was familiar ground. She had served on the ship as a gunnery officer while being transported to the Rim early in her career. To be back aboard after all these years...

A throne dominated the center of the bridge. The Commander kowtowed and said, "Majesty, may I present Commodore Kathleen O'Hare, Imperial Salvage Fleet."

Katy kowtowed the throne. The Crown Prince was younger than she had thought. His long face was framed by a jet-black goatee and the familiar Fu Manchu moustache of a pureblood Mongol. On his head he wore the coronet of the Heir. His white Naval uniform was impeccable with an impressive array of awards and honors on his chest.

His eyes. Her attention was drawn to his eyes. The almond shaped eyes of emerald green that denoted him as a Royal. Katy felt as an insect being examined by a scientist.

"I should think that when one is summoned to the presence of a superior and future sovereign, that one would consider at the very least combing one's hair," his voice was rich, melodious. "Even from one in the service as *laissez-faire* as the Salvage Fleet."

"My apologies, Highness," Katy said. "Your messenger boy was most insistent I report immediately." In the corner of her eye, she saw the stuffy officer stiffen. Good.

"I understand," said the Heir. "They can be a tad over-enthusiastic. To business, then. I come bearing two gifts. The second I will present you tonight at twenty hundred hours local in a banquet aboard this vessel. I extend an invitation to your officers and commanders to attend.

"The first gift comes personally from my mother, the Khan. Behold."

A rating placed a holo emitter on the floor. The image appeared on the floor, a pool of blood, a pair of officer's boots with the blood dripping from the tips of the toes. Legs came into detail, a Naval officer's trousers, deep blue with a gold stripe. A white uniform blouse, pale hands bound behind the body. The shirt was saturated with blood, still flowing freely down the neck. As the head came into view, a hook appeared, impaled from the back of the skull and exiting through the mouth. The eyes of the odious old fat man were rolled back, exposing the whites.

"I assume you recognize my late cousin, former Fleet Admiral Adolphus Astor?" stated the Crown Prince. "He was an ass and rarely allowed in my mother's court. He was found guilty of using his position as a minor Royal for financial gain. The Khan disapproves of such things and had him executed in one of the ancient fashions. She felt you would be interested to know of his dishonor and execution. The Khan told me to say, 'While he deserved death, his blood is not honorable enough to be preserved in my hall.' She said you would understand."

"I do," said Katy. "Please thank your mother for me. If I may take my leave, Crown Prince? I need to return to *Mary Kane* and prepare for your supper."

"Until this evening then, Commodore."

Chapter 21

Tan centered herself and slid into a meditative state as the shuttle carrying her from the *Tranquility* to the *Loki* accelerated away from the hospital ship. She could sense her father's agitation even from this distance. Probably with good reason. She tried to imagine how it must have felt when he lost the connection with Tuhnka.

Tuhnka. His favorite. The one she and all of her sisters knew Father would choose to be *sa-Khan* when he retired. The beautiful blonde woman had always dominated her sisters growing up; indeed, Tuhnka was Tan's best recruiting tool when she approached her other sisters about seizing the title for herself.

Three of her sisters had readily agreed and swore themselves to her. Two had to be eliminated in "accidents". The eighth sister would be afforded the opportunity to join her when Tan returned to Terra at the Crown Prince's side. Or that sister, too, would suffer an accident.

The Crown Prince. Abdul. Her beloved. She had met him while she was just eighteen and starting University in Cairo. He was tall and handsome, the very image of Terran virtue and vitality. There had been no questions three years ago during the naming ceremony when the File Committee had named him Heir. Tan could certainly see why.

A boring social mixer at the Giza Palace was the place of their first meeting. As a distant cousin, she was presented that day to the Khan and welcomed to the family. The societal that night exposed her to generations of hitherto unknown family. Most treated her kindly enough, discussing her being raised as an Intelligence agent and her future plans. A few pandered to her as a new member of the court. One, a lecherous old cousin named Adolphus, a naval officer, had even hinted suggestively about meeting with her after the party. His hand on her hip and backside made his suggestions quite clear. She mentally marked him for future investigations.

The Crown Prince had rescued her from the lech. "Hi, I'm Abdul," he said, taking her elbow and leading her away. In a low voice, he told her, "Cousin Adolphus is the son of a na-Khan. It annoys him muchly that he doesn't have the Khan name. Rather than be proud of his accomplishments, he continually tries this plan and that to impress. It figures, I suppose; his father was Purple File."

The pair became fast friends. He took a great deal of interest in her studies, suggesting from time to time courses she should take and instructors she should work with. As Crown Prince, his duties often took him off world, but his return always meant seeing his mother, the Khan, first, then seeking out his friend Tan.

One evening, he had an unusual request. "Just a blood sample," he said. "Your line is Black File, untouched and untainted by the File Committee for five hundred years. I'd like to see what co-mingling with un-altered DNA has done to the Black line."

The Black line. For reasons obscured through the mists of time, Grandfather Noire ne-Khan had removed his line from the

Imperial line. His daughter, Grandmother Eve na-Kahn/ sa-Khan had written the regulations for the Intelligence line. She created the sa-Khan/ se-Khan titles for Intelligence Masters and their siblings. Each generation was to alternate, male then female. Each was free to choose their own partner or partners; the only stipulation was the children would be raised as special agents and the ultimate agent would be the next sa-Khan.

Tan therefore had seven half-sisters, all roughly the same age as Father had followed the ancient Khalkha tradition and had multiple wives. Only the eight girls his wives bore him would be trained to replace him. Tuhnka had clearly been the favorite.

At age ten, they were taught to kill. Tuhnka had gone first and executed her *Homo Sapiens* victim rather sloppily. When it was Tan's turn, she concentrated and killed the inferior easily enough. Tuhnka had been furious, having always outperformed her sisters and now the least of them had bested her. The two girls immediately became mortal enemies.

Father used the occasion to announce the competition to replace him. Since all his daughters demonstrated the ability to kill, their jobs now were to eliminate or subjugate their competition. Any who would not swear to the future sa-Khan were targets and could be eliminated. Tuhnka had managed to kill one sister right away, strangling her in the night. Tan followed suit before she left for university, encouraging another sister to leap to her death from a tall building.

Abdul came to Tan a few nights after he had extracted the DNA, excited. "Here and here and here," he pointed. Tan understood little about DNA, asking "There and there...what? What is this and what does it mean to me?"

He looked at her in awe. "It is your DNA pattern," he explained. "It means, dear Tan, you are far more than you appear. I would venture to guess your telepathic abilities exceed that even of my mother. You may very well be my equal, or perhaps surpass my abilities in some areas," he said. "With no manipulation, your abilities have far surpassed what would be expected. Surely you have noticed this."

Of course she had. Manipulating her sister to commit suicide had been easy. Sahshood had refused to join Tan's cabal, so Tan altered her to believe suicide was her own option.

Abdul strode back and forth across the room, thinking. "I have a difficult question to ask of you, dearest Tan. You are a hybrid, a natural accident of your lineage's superior breeding and good fortune by your father. It would be a great benefit if your DNA was included in the next line of heirs. There is, of course, the issue with my wife and our heir children. You leave that to me. I am asking you to become my second wife, allow us to harvest your eggs and be mother of the next level of progress in the Imperial line. From *Homo Superior* to *Homo Imperious*. What do you say?"

To be mother of the new line. That appealed to Tan. But she listed her conditions. The Black line was to be taken out of the shadows when he became Emperor, returned to the Imperial Line.

He could cast out useless silver or purple, she didn't care. Her enhanced abilities were to be kept secret; it would be her weapon to use when the time came to replace her father. She would be the one named sa-Kahn when the time arrived.

And he was to have her as his wife. In all ways. In the shadows, of course. That was the Khalkha way for the second wife. But only until his elder wife was disappeared, however he chose. She conceded that she was attracted to the tall, powerful Crown Prince. To take him as her mate would place her that much closer to real power. She was certain when the day of reckoning came, she would have found a way to manipulate this Crown Prince. Just as she had poor Sahshood.

It was done the very next day. She was flown to the Great Temple in Mongolia, the Temple of Angkor Khan. There, in the traditional way, she was married to the Crown Prince. They took her down to the laboratories deep in the mountain and extracted her eggs. She and her new husband enjoyed the gardens of the palace and the vista of the hot Gobi at the walls of the temple.

That evening, he took her to an honored set of chambers high in the temple, the Red Queen's chambers. It was said this was the room the Queen and her husband had first consummated their marriage. The room was a shrine to the greatest Khan to have served the Empire (save for the Founder, of course). There, Abdul and Tan became bonded, as only telepaths could be.

Fifteen years had passed. Tan longed to see her husband. Their plans were nearing fruition. She would become sa-Khan and have the machinery of Intelligence at her fingertips. Soon enough, Abdul's worthless first wife and all her brats would die. He would announce her as his new first wife and their children would be named as successors. The honor of the Black line would be restored. And the future Khan would be superior to all, *Homo Imperious.*

She just had one more task to accomplish.

As soon as she stepped aboard *Loki,* Tan could feel his fury. He was so close to being out of control. Excellent! That was the condition Tan wanted Father to be in. She reached out to him and opened the valve on his virus slightly, just to help him along.

The passageways of *Loki* were lined with helmeted guards. This was new; Father had never felt the need to intimidate her or any of her sisters. They wore standard Imperial combat uniforms, save the helmets which were white globes. Ah, general neutralizers. An average telepath would be unable to penetrate the white shields the guards wore.

What Father didn't know was: Tan was no ordinary telepath. She had always hidden that so well. Today, he would learn just how extraordinary she was.

She strolled through the doorway to his office without a care in the universe. Swartz sat behind his desk. His crimson visage would have terrified Tan, the girl. Today, she suppressed a laugh.

"Where is she!" he demanded. "Don't lie to me, I can tell when you are lying!"

Tan sank into the chair opposite her father and released a bored sigh. "Really, Father? Who or what are you talking about?" She opened the valve just a tiny bit more.

"You damned well know who I am talking about!" he thundered. "What did you do with your sister, Tuhnka? Where is she?"

"What I did was merely follow the rules you laid down when we were children," she explained. "As for where she is…thataway, I assume. I imagine halfway to the sun by now." She waved her hand airily.

"Damn you, Child! I suspended the competition during this situation. What gave you the idea you could disobey and cost me my most valuable agent!" His breathing was becoming labored, his eyes bloodshot.

"Interesting," she thought. "Combine high degrees of stress to the contents of the virus and add my indolence. It's creating physiological damage on its own. Perhaps I will need to study this further."

"You gave no such order, Father. You told Tuhnka she could not kill me while I was in the weakened state after my initial exposure to the *Xian*. Poor Tuhnka followed your orders right up to the end, your perfect little daughter. Sadly for her and for you, I suppose, you gave me no such order." She leaned forward. "I kept the memory of her torment and her death for you. I used one of my servants to defile her before she died. Would you like to see?"

"You BITCH!" He hurled a mental bludgeon at Tan, intent on damaging her. His eyes went wide as she easily caught it and squeezed it to nothing. He found his body frozen, his mind held in by Tan as easily as holding an egg.

"**Foolish little father. Foolish, foolish little man. I have grown far beyond you. I am as a Goddess to you. You could no more bring harm to me than a *chytvurm* could harm a *dyagant*. Sit, little thing.**"

Swartz collapsed back into his chair, still gasping. She entered his mind, finding the blood vessels and neural connections she would need.

"**I originally wanted to kill you as well as Tuhnka. My husband and I discussed it at length. Abdul feels you are more value to us broken, a shell of what you were. I have come to see how you can be of service, as a warning against any *Homo Superior* who may stand against us. And, I will confess, the thought of you living in torment by my hand is far too delicious revenge to pass up.**

Enjoy this moment, Father. It is the last pleasure you will ever feel."

She manipulated the nerve endings, then opened the small capillaries in his head. She planted the torture, rape and death of Tuhnka in his virus, so it would appear at random intervals. She withdrew and watched as her father twitched and slumped in his chair. The right side of his face began to sag, drool to ooze from the corner of his mouth. Blood trailed from his right ear. His eyes closed for a moment, then opened, focused on his daughter. Unintelligible grunts and growls directed at her. Oh, she could look in his head, she supposed, to see if he had anything interesting to say. But she wasn't really interested.

"Salinas!" Tan called. The young girl entered the sa-Khan's office. To her credit, she didn't visibly react to the slumping sa-Khan. Tan swept the girl's mind quickly, pleased with what she found. The girl was *Homo Superior* and of good breeding. Swartz had trained her well. She would bear watching as she continued her training. Perhaps even becoming an aide for Tan, the role Father was training her for.

"**Notify *Tranquility*. I believe my father has had a stroke and needs immediate medical attention. Instruct *Loki's* crew I am assuming control of both the ship and the local situation. Ready my shuttle; I will need to report to this to the Crown Prince.**"

"**Yes, Ma'am.**" Salinas kowtowed and turned to leave.

"**Salinas, before you go.**"

The girl turned back to the *se-Khan.*

"**Do you have any issues with all of this?**"

"**No, Ma'am.**"

"**Then you will swear your fealty to me and take the Bond of Obedience.**"

"**Of course.**" The teen knelt before Tan and opened her mind. "**I swear my obedience to you, Mistress, for now and all time. My life is now yours.**"

Tan found the cluster of nerves in Salinas' head and placed her clamp upon it. Now, should Salinas attempt to disobey or deceive her mistress, Tan would know about it instantly. It would be the girl's death. Further, Tan copied the virus and placed it in her head.

"**I have placed a virus shell within your head. I want you to examine it and understand it for what it is. Should I suspect you, I will open the valve and subject you to punishment you cannot imagine. I have already used it to destroy my sister and my father; do not think I will hesitate to use it on you.**

Now, go and do my bidding."

Chapter 22

Holo-emitters. That was the only explanation.

Katy stood at the doorway of the banquet hall aboard the *Ashira*. "HANGAR BAY 4" read the sign above the passageway door. But once she passed through the portal, she was magically transported a hundred thousand light years away.

It was a circular room, all in ivory and gold. The ceiling arched five hundred feet and flowering vines climbed the arches, filled the air with their perfume. Beyond the arches, was a cerulean sky tinged with cerise, a slate mountain rose to Katy's left. Dusty silver clouds hung on the horizon. A long, slender beast leapt from the mountain, bat wings and sinewy body flapping slowly as it circled the venue, then turned and flew off into the horizon.

A low buzz filled the resplendent room. Officers both from the Imperial Fleet and her own Salvage Fleet filled it to capacity. All the ship Captains and their senior officers mingled; the royal blue of the fleet circulating with the mixed bag of her officers. She suppressed a chuckle as Lieutenant Commander Bret Johnson, her scout officer who had found the *Xian,* strolled by. It was clear that he had either gained weight or his dress uniform had shrunk. Curiously, his dress uniform was that of an Army Bomber Pilot. She decided maybe she should take a closer look at his records.

Colonel Cavner and his son were dashing in their black and green Army uniforms. Katy had field promoted the younger Cavner for his outstanding work in searching and securing *Xian*. His proud father had personally pinned the now *Major* Cavner's eagle and saber insignia.

The *major domo* stepped next to her. "Impressive, yes?" he said. "It is a replication of the throne room on Dionides Seven, a favored world of the royal family. The birds and insects..." Katy noticed both fluttering and flying about..." aren't part of the program. The Crown Prince keeps a small menagerie onboard for just such occasions.

"The Crown Prince has been delayed, Commodore, for just a few minutes. Personal business, I was told. If you'll be patient, the ceremony should start momentarily."

Katy used the time to study the crowd. More than forty alien races were represented amongst the military officers present. She wasn't surprised, with more than one hundred twenty-five thousand worlds and colonies. Katy would have been more surprised if there were fewer aliens serving in the fleet. Her heart swelled with pride, at the center of the Empire were her people, the Terran people.

Unifier of the galaxy.

The *major domo* was at her elbow again. "Ma'am, the Crown Prince is ready. If you would come with me?" He led her to a spot on the edge of the dais.

A fanfare filled the room. Katy and the rest of the room snapped to attention, facing the center of the stage. A bright spot of light revealed the Crown Prince in a blazing white uniform with a red sash and a chest full of medals. A plain steel saber hung from his hip, a steel ring circled his head. He drew his saber and raised it to his officers. At once, everyone fell to a knee. "My Khan," they chanted. "I offer my service and my life to your Empire."

"I honor your service," he replied. "I vow to honor the lives you offer to my Empire." He replaced his saber and the crowd of officers stood. "I bring you all greeting from my mother, the Empress Annabelle Lind Russolov Khan. She asked me to recognize the efforts of the First Salvage Fleet. You are tasked a difficult mission, to clean up the battlefield after the fleet defeats the enemies of the Empire. My mother wishes me to express her heartfelt gratitude to each of you. The gentle and respectful ways you recover and return our fallen soldiers and naval personnel heralds of the greatest service anyone does for our Empire. In this action here at the Joeanmika system, you have further brought honor to your service with the rescue of nearly thirty thousand civilians, both citizens and Terrans who live on the fringes of the Empire along the Rim. Well done."

The Naval officers applauded the Salvage officers.

"My mother, the Khan, has made one of the foundations of her Empire to be redemption and forgiveness. Too often in the Empire's past, we have rolled over citizens and races with no consideration for their sacrifice to the Empire. Indeed, in the past, corruption and graft within the Royal family has created disgrace for honored servants to the Empire.

"Thirty standard years ago, a distant cousin of mine accused a fine young officer of disobedience and cowardice. This officer pursued an enemy into a nebula with orders to herd the nemesis out of the nebula where my cousin, seeking glory for himself, would destroy the foe. Through guile and cunning, she was able to destroy her adversary but thereby embarrassing my cousin. This officer was tried and convicted to death for disobedience and cowardice. By regulation, she was presented to the Khan to order her execution. Instead, the young Khan chose to use the woman as a demonstration of her trust in her officers over family.

"While she couldn't restore the officer to the Navy, she restored the officer's rank and assigned her to the Salvage fleet. That officer has led you with distinction and honor.

"My mother had watched this officer throughout her career. She has decided it is time to right the wrong done to her so long ago. Commodore Katy O'Hare, attend your Khan!"

Katy braced and marched before the Crown Prince and saluted. He returned the salute and announced, "Commodore O'Hare. The Empress, having reviewed your records both before and after your disgrace, has issued an exoneration of the dishonor of which you stood accused. In light of your service to her and to the Empire, the Empress has ordered you to return to Naval Service and be promoted two levels. Further, she has reached back to our ancestors to revive a title. You are now ascended to Noyan-Behi. In standard, it translates to General-Honored Lady of the Court."

Stunned, Katy stood stiffly while the Crown Prince removed the single ringed star of her rank and replaced it with the holo-enhanced galaxy and crossed swords. She accepted the Crown

Prince's salute, then took a knee as he drew his saber and tapped her three times, declaring her new title.

Katy proudly faced her fellow officers. "Officers!" called the Crown Prince. "I present the Noyan-Behi, Vice Admiral Katy O'Hare. Salute!" The entire room raised their arms and chanted, "hoooOOOO! hoooOOOO! hoooOOOO!"

The *major domo* organized them into the receiving line quickly and efficiently. As the Crown Prince's honored guest, she stood to the right of His Majesty, receiving the salutes and congratulations of all the guests. As Doctor Ho-Bar approached, Katy saw tears flowing from the corners of his eyes. Protocol be damned, she accepted his salute and fierce hug.

At that moment, a commotion came from behind them. "Ah, my second wife has finally arrived," announced the Khan. "She refused to appear unless she was properly attired. Women!" The whole of the room laughed, including Katy. A fanfare sounded and everyone in the room stood and faced an entryway behind the dais.

Katy barely suppressed a gasp.

Tan, lofty and regal, strode into the room. She was wearing a faceted headpiece of dark matter that flowed around her neck, followed the lines of her slender build down to the hem of her black dress. Her gown was off one shoulder and split to her hip on the other side. She took the Crown Prince's proffered hand and acknowledged the applause from the congregated officers.

Katy maintained her presence, while her mind processed what had just been revealed. *Tan? Second wife of the future Emperor? Why all the secrecy? By law and tradition, a Khalkha warrior could have as many wives as he desired. As the God-King of the Khalkha, he had no need to conceal multiple wives. Why Tan? I know she is an outstanding agent of Imperial Intelligence. Why would she forsake her future in Intelligence to be the concubine of an Emperor? Especially as Second Wife. The heirs were selected from the First Wife. What am I missing here?*

The line had dwindled when the *Major Domo* announced seating for supper. Katy followed the Crown Prince and Tan to the central table. As his honored guest, Katy was seated to his right.

"I must apologize for the tardiness of my wife for your honors, Vice Admiral," the Crown Prince stated. "She was summoned for a family emergency."

"Family emergency?" puzzled Katy. "I was not aware Agent Tan had family in my fleet."

"No, I imagine you didn't," Abdul said. "Tan is exceptionally skilled at the art of concealment and deception."

"My Father appears to have suffered a stroke," said Tan. "I oversaw his transfer to the *Tranquility* for treatment before reporting to my husband for your ceremony."

"You should have stayed with your father," scolded Katy. "Who is he so I can check on his condition?"

Tan stared at her for a moment, then stated, "My father is the *sa-Khan,* Imperial Intelligence Master Swartz. Thank you for your kindness, Admiral. However, the situation is well in hand. The head physician believes the combination of the situation on the *Xian* and the disappearance of my sister was sufficient stress to cause a capillary stroke in the left hemisphere of his brain. While he is certain to survive, there is the question as to his abilities to resume his duties."

"You have a sister?" Katy asked.

"I believe that is what I said, Vice Admiral," Tan's replied icily. "In fact, I had seven sisters. Three are now dead or, in Tuhnka's case, missing, presumed dead."

"Where was she last seen?" asked Katy. "I'll have a search begun immediately."

"*Loki* has been searching for her since her disappearance, Admiral," said Tan. "She is an Imperial Intelligence agent and a telepath. As such, the *sa-Kahn* has had as many agents as he could spare searching for her psionically. Thus far, we have had no sign of her. I can only assume we should declare her dead as soon as the traditional ninety-six hours have passed. The strain appears to have felled Father."

"Another reason for having my second wife present, Vice Admiral," stated the Crown Prince. "I am placing her in charge of Intelligence for the *Xian* operation. I have sent word to the Khan; I am certain she will name Tan *sa-Khan* permanently."

How convenient for Tan, thought Katy. *I placed her in the system, her husband is the future Emperor Khan, her sister disappears, and her father is incapacitated. Were I a suspicious woman...*

Katy vowed to keep a close eye on her former officer.

In their private quarters, Tan had a pair of servants help her removed the elaborate headpiece and jeweled collar before entering the bed chamber where her husband waited. He had already undressed and was in bed, waiting. Seductively, Tan removed the tight gown, revealing herself to her husband. She slid between the cool sheets and began the slow act of lovemaking to him.

As telepaths, their foreplay was more than touching and caressing. As their tongues wrestled and hands sought sensitive spots they knew of each other, their minds intertwined, fondling and touching with an intimacy a non-telepath could never understand.

They joined, physically. In the deepest reaches of her mind, Tan watched, almost clinically, the excited state of her husband's mind. She was waiting, as a trapdoor spider waits, for the moment that he was fully distracted by her body. Then she would surreptitiously place the virus in her lover's mind, concealed where he would not easily find it.

And thus, she would ensure that when the time was right, she, Tan *sa-Khan,* wife of the Emperor, would in fact rule the Empire.

He was nearly there. She writhed her body beneath him appropriately, making the expected moans and cries. His movements were frantic, in another few seconds...

His hand was on her throat. She couldn't breathe. Moreover, he commanded her not to breath. She couldn't dislodge his grip, either his hand or his mind.

"Foolish bitch!" his voice filled her head. He towered over her now, a mass of black, terrifying Tan, greater than any black she could imagine, the terror greater than what she felt when she first encountered *Xian*.

"Did you truly believe you could conceal anything from me? This?" She watched as he crushed the virus she had tried to plant. **"Clearly, you have forgotten who you are and who I am. Yes, you are the hybrid, a mind more powerful than any before in your line. Our children will be the future of the species, not to mention the future of the Empire."**

But, I am the Khan, heir to the throne. I am the God-King of Terra. While you were learning your silly little techniques to interrogate, terrorize and investigate, I was learning how to rule an Empire. Including how to rule my wives."

Silly cousin, do you really think I didn't know it was all an act? Your professed love for me? Did you not consider that as Khan, I have been taught to watch for plans within plans, to seek out treachery and deceit, to keep my friends close, but my enemies closer? And how much closer could I keep my most dangerous enemy than to make you my wife."

Tan could feel the grey of unconsciousness forming at the corners of her mind. She had to escape! If he held her in this grasp for only seconds longer, he would kill her!

"Mercy, Husband, I beg of you!" she cried.

She felt his clamps secure over her nerves, not asking for her permission or giving her the chance to take the vow of obedience.

"Here is my mercy. You are bound to me now, whether you will it or not. You shall obey me without question. You cannot conceal anything from me. You will do anything required of you to protect me and my Empire, even if that means your own life. Do you understand?"

"Yes…Master."

He released all at once, his hand from her throat, his grip from her mind. He filled her to his pleasure, then rolled off and made himself comfortable while she struggled to recover.

"You know, I have discovered the secret of your Vice Admiral O'Hare," he told her. **"It is a rare condition, seen only in one of several hundred or perhaps thousands of her kind. The polite term is "esper blind". It is not a defect but rather a natural defense some of the *Sapiens* developed naturally. In historical records, Yuri, the Red Queen's *Sapiens* husband was esper blind. It is recorded in her diaries that it was the characteristic that drew her to him. Disgusting. Bad enough to mix *Superior* blood with inferior *Sapiens*, but at the time, she had little option."**

Recovered, he began to touch his wife again. **"I believe she will need careful watching,"** he told Tan, **"and I will demonstrate further my superiority over you by using the very skills your father was incapable of teaching you. Already, she views us as allies. By the end of tomorrow, your Vice Admiral will be eating out of my hand, willing to take the loyalty oath, should I require it."**

Chapter 23

"Good morning, Admiral O'Hare. Ship's time is zero five zero-zero. This is your requested wake up call. Good morning, Admiral O'Hare..."

Katy croaked, "All right, alright, I'm awake." The message stopped immediately. She swung her legs over the edge of her bed, scrubbing the sleep from her face. The computer had picked up on her promotion. Good work for the tug's computer; usually *Mary Kane's* would have to be reminded two or three times of such things.

Her door chimed, followed by a discreet knock. "Admiral O'Hare?" a voice called from the door comm.

Oh, for the love of... Katy thought darkly. She donned her robe and called, "Enter!"

The Bauc'td entered, its hundreds of tentacles arranged to simulate a bipedal form. Bauc'td s were natural mimics, so its skin had taken on the hues of an Imperial officer uniform. Around its neck it wore a standard translator. Smaller tentacles on its "head" imitated eye stalks. They fixed on Katy as it said, "Greetings, Admiral O'Hare. I am Commander Thrxxk. The Crown Prince has assigned me to be your Chief of Staff until such time you are able to research and assemble your own staff. This first order of business..."

"Wait, wait, wait..." Katy said, waving a hand. "I just woke up. Give me a minute to wake up, have a cuppa."

The Bauc'td's *faux* eye stalks fixed on her. "A cup of what, Admiral?"

Katy wondered if it were possible to throttle the alien.

"Commander Thrxxk, my alarm went off thirty seconds ago." Katy told hi/r. "Terrans my age need a few minutes to wake up, have a nice cup of tea, perhaps a biscuit and kipper before charging into the day. So, before you start on my schedule, would you please fetch me a cup of tea, with two sugars and a squeeze of lemon? Then I solemnly swear to wake up enough to pay attention to your report."

The Bauc'td hesitated, then crept out the door. S/he returned minutes later bearing a heavy white mug, with a lazy tendril of steam wafting from its wide mouth. "As you ordered, Admiral, with two sugars," Commander Thrxxk said, handing her the mug.

"And a wee bit of lemon?" Katie asked.

"Yes, Ma'am."

Katy sipped the mug, exhaling loudly. "Oh, Commander Thrxxk, what you lack in Terran understanding you more than make up for with this cup of tea. Proceed, please."

"Thank you, Ma'am," Thrxxk said. "I will adjust your schedule five minutes for your "cuppa". When you are finished, you will change for forty-five minutes of exercise at the ship's gymnasium…"

"Hold on, Commander. Forty-five minutes in the ship's gymnasium?" Katy asked.

"Yes, Ma'am," S/he answered. "I have based your schedule on the Crown Prince's. Daily, he exercises forty-five minutes. He alternates from weight training to *Shakti* and finishes with a five-mile swim."

"Problem one, Thrxxk," Katy said. "The Crown Prince lives on a Command Carrier. *Mary Kane* is a salvage tug. We have no gymnasium or swimming pool. I haven't a clue what *Shakti* is."

"It is a meditative form of..."

"I don't care," Katy snapped. "I get enough exercise for a sixty-seven-year-old woman. Next?"

The Bauc'td's tentacles writhed as s/he continued. "Ten minutes for toilet, five minutes for your shower..."

"Ten minutes for toilet, five minutes for shower," mimicked Katy. "Tell me, have you the time I don my knickers as well?"

The Bauc'td regarded his/her schedule. "Not specifically, Ma'am," Thrxxk said. "I believe that falls under 'dressing.'"

"How long?"

"Nine and one-half minutes."

"I assume the half minute is give or take?" Katy asked.

"No ma'am. It is an exact time," Thrxxk said.

Katy sighed. "Understand, Commander, I am bound to be a wee bit different from serving the Crown Prince," she said. "Put this on your schedule. The Admiral will awake at five a.m. ship's time. Forty-five minutes later you may join me in the wardroom for breakfast, after which we will go over my schedule. Understand?"

"No, Ma'am," her aide said. "Breakfast will be served here forty-five minutes after your wake-up call. It would be…inappropriate for you to dine with your underlings. Also, given the complexities of your duties, you will have little time for socialization in the morning."

"Well, then, seeing how I'm going to dine in the wardroom this morning, I would suggest you start your briefing now," said Katy. "Me? I'm taking a shower." She padded into her bathroom.

Katy was pleased to see the Bauc'td had laid out her clothes for the day (including her knickers.) She was less pleased to see her breakfast sitting on the desk. At least s/he poured another tea and ordered oatmeal and bangers. Bowing to the inevitable, she sat and ate, reading the pad s/he'd left of her morning briefing. Finished, she noticed Thrxxk had laid out a uniform jacket rather than Katy's preferred sweater. Grumbling, she grabbed the jacket and left for the bridge.

"Attention! Admiral on the bridge!" Thrxxk's voice carried across *Mary Kane's* command center. The whole room stomped to attention. Before Katy could order them to ease, Commander Thrxxk ordered, "Render honors!" All the officers and ratings kowtowed to Katy. Mortified, Katy looked to Thrxxk, who was bent over as well. Her mouth felt dry as she squeaked "Rise."

The bustle of the bridge returned to normal. Katy stopped at her place at the holo tank and sighed. Her old comfortable chair had been replaced with a more ornate chair, practically a throne, with a high back and ornate scrollwork. The padding was absent, as tradition demanded. The person who occupied the chair was to be honored with the throne, but always reminded while sitting uncomfortably to pay attention to what was happening around them.

Jhon Bosley was waiting by her new post, wearing Captain's Falcons now. Katy had promoted him to fill many of her roles, as her duties would be changing. He had earned the job, despite his protestations. Those were her own Falcons on his collar.

"Status, Captain?"

"*Mary Kane* is operating at expected efficiency," Bosley reported. "Engineer Otero is running Engineering while Engineer Diezac is aboard *Xian*. We are currently supporting the assembly of salvage raft four. *China Girl* is completing rigging of raft three. He expects to depart within thirty-six hours. *Respite* reports the first of the honored dead are ready for transport to their homes and the Necropolis on Terra. They ask when you will be prepared for the departure ceremony and which ship has the honor of transporting the remains?"

"My compliments to Captain Lanes of *Respite*," stated Katy. "Notify *Taiho;* he has earned the honor of transporting the hearse to Terra; frigates *Star Cloud* and *Shrike* will serve as escorts. The ceremony will be in seventy-two hours. Please send word to *Ashira;* extend my personal invitation to the Crown Prince to attend the ceremony."

"Yes, Admiral."

For the next hour, the commanders made their reports from the salvage fleet. Progress was back on track now that *Xian* was stable. Scouts continued their sector by sector investigation, searching for remains and salvageable debris. The planets and major moons had been checked for survivors. None were found; each celestial body was uninhabitable for Terrans. As many as two hundred of the red heads were found on one rocky planet. Katy had ordered *Valiant,* her medium carrier, to attack the planet. The carrier launched its entire attack wing, bombing and strafing the clumps of red heads on the planet. It was great sport for the fighter crews, and various games were created amongst themselves to exterminate any sign of the unnatural enemy. Within a standard day, the planet was barren again, now bearing scorch marks and bloodied pools.

A decision on the survivors aboard *Xian* had not been reached. Despite of the loss of Intelligence Master Swartz *sa-Khan* and his daughter, Special Agent Tuhnka, the agents of Intelligence had completed the survey of survivors. Results were discouraging. Seventeen thousand males were found, cruelly hung from the walls in the cargo hold, the spikes in their skulls controlling them. Less than a third maintained sentience, although all were living.

For the women, the situation was far worse. Thirteen thousand survivors were aboard. Nine thousand had been altered, arms and legs amputated, "unnecessary" organs removed. Only enough brain stem remaining to service their uteri, being used as incubators for red heads. The remaining four thousand were held in chemically induced comas, waiting for their alterations and impregnation. Fifteen hundred pubescent girls were amongst the comatose victims. They were being pumped full of growth mediums and hormones to accelerate their maturation, doomed to serve as their sisters in the tanks where they lay, growing more red heads.

The same chemicals that held them in a coma destroyed their sentience.

Thirty thousand Terran civilians, most of whom were beyond saving. Katy had sent her report to the Imperial Council and awaited its reply.

The Salvage Fleet morning reports were complete. Katy settled back in her new chair but found it too uncomfortable. Commander Thrxxk was making an odd noise, as though s/he was trying to clear his/her throat. "Yes Commander Thrxxk," Katy acknowledged.

"Admiral, you still have the morning Naval briefing to complete…" Thrxxk began, holding out the pad.

"Excellent!" Katy exclaimed. "Captain Bosley, carry on. I'll be in the observer's pylon reviewing my report." She leapt from the rough chair and bolted for the elevator at the rear of the bridge.

The observer's pylon was a relic installed in a more romantic time when Captains would observe the salvage from its privacy. Rising four decks behind the bridge, the station at the top was a clear dome with a pair of work stations. Across the fleet, the observer's pylons were in disuse, though on *Mary Kane* it had become a hideout for senior officers when they wanted peace and quiet.

Engineer Diezac had installed a simple lock from the inside so whoever was in the dome could work uninterrupted.

With the Bauc'td continually in her ear all morning, Katy decided she needed a break. She dropped the pad into a slot at the work station, settled back into the comfortable chair and listened to the report while staring at the stars. It was dry, technical stuff, troop movements through the Empire, supply inventories for the nearest sector, political happenings along this part of the Rim and back on Terra.

The minutia an Admiral needed at her fingertips.

A discreet tapping on the elevator door. *Shave and a haircut*... The ancient tap still used covertly by Terrans since aliens never seemed to figure it out. The bristly hair of Jhon Bosley appeared at the door, then his lopsided grin. "Mind if I join you, Admiral?" he asked.

"What's up, Jhon?" Katy asked. "Trouble with my new Chief of Staff?"

"Nah, I've worked around Bauc'td s before," Jhon replied. "Nosey little buggers and they're none too bright on the uptake. This one is sharp enough. Except I may have had to beat it down a bit, reminding him who is a Captain and who is a Commander. S/he's sitting quietly in a corner of the bridge, watching the elevator for you to appear. I think s/he has duty separation anxiety."

They chuckled. "Jhon, that whole stand up and bow thing this morning…" she began.

He waved his hand dismissively. "Your Chief of Staff came up this morning and briefed us on how to approach and the proper etiquette when one is in the vicinity of an Honored Lady of the Court and an Admiral," he said. His eye got a faraway look for a second. "You know, we would have done it even if s/he hadn't insisted. The whole fleet is proud of you, Katy."

"Then why do I feel like the other boot is set to drop?" she asked. "This whole situation stinks. I don't trust this Crown Prince any further than I could throw him. Tan has become a complete stranger to me. And the thirty thousand…" her voice trailed off.

"Yeah," Jhon sighed heavily. "What are we going to do with them, Katy? There isn't a facility big enough for them all in the Empire. And the last time I spoke with Dan Diezac, he told me flat out the *Xian* will never leave the system. He's too damaged to translate from normal space to otherspace and back again. Even using four heavy tugs won't do the job. What's going to happen to all those poor people? We can't just leave them aboard a dying ship."

"I don't know either," she said. "Listen Jhon, you're Captain of the *Mary Kane* now. Whatever you do, you must first protect him and the crew. This whole situation is going sideways on me right now. I need to know whatever happens, you swear to me you'll take care of this ship and my fleet. Even if it means leaving me behind. Understand?"

"Katy…" Jhon began.

"Katy nothing. Promise me, Jhon," she ordered. "If anything happens, get *Mary Kane* and the rest of the fleet out of here. Pick a muster point and transmit it quietly throughout the fleet. Don't cause a commotion; tell them it's updating the contingency plan. Heck, it is updating the contingency plan."

"Have you looked at what the Crown Prince brought with him?" Jhon asked. "Christ, it's a full fracking Battle Fleet! What kind of chance do we stand against that?"

"That's why you need to get the message out quickly," Katy said. "Pick a jump point, transmit it to the fleet."

The comm buzzed. "Admiral, the Crown Prince wishes to speak with you." Even through the comm, Thrxxk's voice was irritating.

"Very well, send the message up here to my station," Katy ordered.

"Admiral, protocol when communicating with the Crown Prince…," the Bauc'td started to protest.

"My station, Commander," Katy ordered.

A foot tall holo of the Crown Prince appeared on Katy's work station. He startled, surprised the Admiral hadn't shown the proper obedience to him, standing, bowing and such. Well, no matter.

"Admiral, wonderful to see you again," he said. "And hard at work, too. Excellent. I so admire an officer who is diligent with her work. I've decided I need to look the *Xian* over myself, get a firsthand experience with what's happened on that damned ship. I will expect you, your engineer aboard and your Doctor Ho-Bar to accompany us."

"What of Colonel Cavner and his troops?" asked Katy.

"I sent them off this morning," the Crown Prince replied. "With my Battle Group, I don't think we need to worry about defense. I have adequate troops with me and the Colonel's unit is needed elsewhere. Shall we say after lunch? Thirteen hundred hours?"

"We'll be there, Highness," Katy replied.

"Excellent. I'll see you aboard *Xian* then, Admiral." The tiny hologram popped out.

"Get that message sent out now, Jhon," she ordered.

Chapter 24

Five hundred Imperial Marines in full combat dress snapped to attention as the trio of assault shuttles bearing the Crown Prince entered the *Xian's* landing bay. Two were decoys. Even surrounded by a full Battle Fleet, the Heir could be none too careful.

Engineer Diezac and his team had done an amazing job restoring the bay. Katy had observed the best engineers always found a way to keep their spaces neat and organized. No matter what the fate of a ship, a good engineer would insure the vessel was clean and ship shape. More than once she had boarded a ship that had clearly taken time to die. There might be a hole through the primary hull or the engines neatly sheared off by an enemy. Touring the hulk, they would nearly always find engineering spaces neat and organized until the engineers sat down and died.

Such had not been the case on *Xian*. The enemy abandoned the dying ship and its cargo to the cruel hands of fate. Diezac's pride insisted that even this ship, condemned to the scrapper, would be in as good of shape as could be managed.

More Marines emerged from two assault doors just opened and the Crown Prince exited the shuttle to Katy's right, dressed in a gleaming gold battle armor. On one side and just behind him was Tan, similarly dressed, save her armor was black.

"Majesty," Katy greeted the Heir with a deep kowtow. "Welcome aboard *Xian*. My officers and I are prepared for your tour."

"Very well." Abdul said. "Just a quick tour of engineering. I am most interested in seeing the cargo of this ship."

Katy had Engineer Diezac lead the tour of the engineering section. Clearly, he was pleased with the progress his small band of engineers had accomplished in the weeks since they'd boarded. While not gleaming as on the *Mary Kane,* he had made extensive use of the available slave pool to clean the section. Burned and scorched walls had been scrubbed, panels restored, dangling wiring and ducts repaired or removed.

"I've had to shut down the breeder reactors because of the damage caused to the system by the units on fire when we arrived," Diezac explained. "Hence, we are unable to draw any power from them. The ship's main power plant is functional, but barely. As such, we've closed off as many sections of the ship as possible to conserve power."

"Impressive," complimented the Heir. "But you say for all this, the ship is unsalvageable. Why?"

"The *Xian's* structural integrity has been grossly compromised," Diezac expounded. "His keel is fractured in a dozen places. Two are full displacements, probably when we pulled him to this orbit. Even if we were to cradle the *Xian* in a full tug rig and use four fleet tugs, there is only a slim chance he might be able to handle the shearing forces of entering otherspace. He would most certainly not survive an exit. Either way, entering or exiting, the destruction of the *Xian* passing through the space fold would also destroy the tugs."

"I will, of course, have a team of my own engineers come aboard to validate your assessment," the Crown Prince decided.

"It will be an honor for myself and my team," Dan answered.

"Let's continue the tour, please," ordered the Crown Prince.

His marines led the way, unerringly forward at a fast march. They reached the male captives hanging from their harnesses, their lives still controlled by the derelict ship's computer. In unison, the captives inhaled and exhaled. Clearly the Heir had been briefed and prepared for the unsettling noise of thousands of lungs filling and emptying.

Katy noticed two out of three men had a red "X" painted on their chest. She pointed it out. "My agents have determined these…beings have lost their sentience," stated Tan. "They are effectively brain dead, a drain on ship's resources. Your Doctor Ho-Bar refuses to disconnect them and allow them to die."

"What agent Tan fails to mention," Ho-Bar countered, "is our instrumentation shows a low level of brain activity. By law, as long as there is brain activity, I am required to treat them as patients."

"Convenient to ease your conscience, I'm sure," Tan purred. "I remind you, my agents have been inside each of their brains. I can assure you, *Doctor,* they are as dead as the Eighth Emperor."

"Enough," said the Crown Prince. "Each of these are Terrans and as such are under my protection. This fellow, for instance…" He motioned at a blond man staring blankly cross the hall. "…His name is Lars Thomas. He lost his wife and three sons during the attack on his homeworld of Saiphron. He has two daughters that he saw captured. He desperately wants to know where his daughters are." The Crown Prince patted the catatonic man's cheek. "Have courage, young Lars," he said. "I promise you, we'll find your daughters and return them to you." He strode down the passageway toward the bridge.

Katy stopped before Lars Thomas. She looked into his ice blue eyes, searching for a sign of life. *Are you in there?* She wondered. *Can't you show me some sign, any sign, that you are still alive?* His dead eyes stayed fixed, he inhaled sharply with the rest of the men hanging around him. Frightened, Katy scurried away.

The next stop was at the chambers known as the nursery. Abdul moved in silence between the rows of the breeding tanks, scarcely looking in them. He stopped every dozen yards and tried to read the minds of the victims. After the third such stop, he shrugged and walked across the room.

Tan walked slowly behind her husband, her hands clasped comfortably behind her back. She wore a small, satisfied smile; the cat proudly showing her master the dead mouse she had caught for his pleasure.

He entered the inner sanctum where the unmodified, comatose women were stored. Katy was glad the tubs were filled with the noxious chemical clouds the slaves insisted were necessary to sustain the mutilated women.

The first time she toured this section of the ship, Katy had been violently ill and nearly gave in to the mind-numbing call of the whiskey back aboard the *Mary Kane*. It would provide her relief, she knew. But only until the alcohol faded. Then the nightmare of the maimed women would return, she knew. She set her jaw and marched briskly through the chamber, looking neither left nor right

The slaves identified the area as "medical storage." It stored the unmutilated bodies of the women destined to replace the ones in the nursery. A large bank to her right contained the children, though growth mediums and hormone therapy had accelerated the growth of the youngest children well into puberty.

"Here!" called the excited Crown Prince. "The children of Lars Thomas!" He waved with excitement for Katy to come see. On wooden legs, she prepared herself to view what the monsters had done to the children.

Two teen-aged looking girls lay naked side by side on the shelf. Their hips were widening, and small breasts had formed. They looked to be sleeping, though the wires coming from behind their bald heads revealed their brains were responding to the directives of a mechanical god. They looked so at peace, despite the obscenities being done to them.

"I can barely read them," the Crown Prince said softly. "They see themselves back on their home, doing their chores and playing. It is a continuous loop of the same vision. I should suppose it keeps them relaxed."

"We do much the same during regeneration bathes," Doctor Ho-Bar's voice was equally soft, as though not to disturb the sleeping children. "We find the patient recovers quicker when not exposed to reliving whatever got them into the tank. Calm, happy dreams also make the time go quicker, studies have revealed."

"So they are not suffering," Katy asked.

"In my opinion, for now, no," the Doctor replied. "They are simply reliving the same dream over and over."

"Is this what is happening to…them?" Katy asked, nodding her head towards the nursery.

"No," Ho-Bar said, "When they were lobotomized, that portion of the brain was removed."

Katy slumped. Reality of the situation was far worse than she could have imagined. The high collar of her jacket was too restrictive, she needed to vomit. "Pardon me, Highness," she gagged.

Outside in the passageway, she emptied her stomach. Still the heaves came. In forty-five years in space, she had never encountered anything like this. Terran children reduced to feed and breed stock.

A kind hand patted her back. The Crown Prince extended his other hand and helped Katy back to her feet. They found a washroom where Katy could rinse her mouth and wipe her face.

"Now you see what I've known for many years, Admiral O'Hare," said the Heir. "There are wars coming. Civil wars of sorts. Where the Terrans of the past will encounter the Terrans of the future. Not only does it mean the survival of our species, but the very survival of the Empire. Come, it's time for you to learn the truth and this washroom is hardly the place."

He escorted her down the passageway to the auxiliary control room. They were joined by Agent Tan, Engineer Diezac and Doctor Ho-Bar. Armed marines locked the chamber and guarded the door.

"Three thousand years ago, my grandfather and Founder of our Empire, Angkor Khan, struck upon an idea to expand the Empire. The first war with the Hecht was at its conclusion, his Empire had secured the secret of ship-sized otherspace generators. Prior to this, expensive vessels known as rail drives, were used to access otherspace. Clearly, this was a dangerous time to be growing an Empire; our ships were built with the rail ships in mind. Therefore, they were small and the only way we defeated the Hecht was through courage and cunning."

"Following the war, Grandfather had an idea. He mounted laboratories and sleeper ships on the rail ships and sent them deep into the galaxy, under the aegis of creating dozens and dozens of Terran colonies far flung across the Galaxy. Each would establish a Terran outpost, a small version of our Empire, if you will. This way, conquest would be easier. Why fight an enemy when you can develop allies across the universe with a few strands of parent DNA?

"Fifteen ships were sent out. Already, we are finding pockets of success as we move Spinward. Three Terran-based Empires have formed and are all too pleased to be reunited with their ancestors.

"Secret records show that Angkor banished one of his enemies, the Shurkorov family, with a preprogramed rail ship. The anticipation was they would be sent so far away, we should not encounter them for fifteen thousand years. Adding to Angkor's plan, the DNA they were supplied was faulty. It should have created a substandard series of species rather than the advanced ones we have encountered here. I for one, would have never imagined them using female Terrans to gestate and incubate their young. Further, the development of their Feloid warriors..." The Crown Prince shuddered.

"You mentioned wars," stated Katy. "This war with the Sudahar is certainly of concern. But they had to steal ships to journey here. And already we have demonstrated the cunning and strength of the Terran warrior. With the Sudahar dismissed, what other wars are we facing?"

"Admiral O'Hare," The Crown Prince said. "When I was a child, my siblings and I were taken throughout our Empire, exposing us to all of the lifeforms one of us would ultimately rule. Observing their cultures, learning about them while they learned about us. I found I am to one day lead a growing, vibrant Empire, ever advancing and becoming better than what we as individuals are. That was part of Angkor Khan's plan.

"When we were seven, we took a journey up to the Neanderthal Valley on Terra where we were shown an ancient species, precursors to your species, *Homo Neanderthal*. Around thirty-one thousand years ago, their species died off, replaced with a new and more advanced species, *Homo Sapiens*. There is evidence that shows the two species lived side by side for many years until the Neanderthal died off, most likely at the hands of the Sapiens.

"That is the nature of things, Katy. When the time comes, the older, less able species will have been overwhelmed and replaced by the new, vibrant species. We already have the new species on hand, the *Homo Superior,* created by none other than my grandfather, the Great Khan himself.

"I have been so fortunate recently to have seen the future. My heirs will be of a new species, the species that will lead my Empire for the next ten thousand years, perhaps longer. *Homo Imperious*. But we still have the pesky problem of our ancestors."

"Ah, I understand," Katy said, "You want us inferior *Homo Sapiens* to die off like the Neanderthal. This would leave plenty of room for the *Superior* and the *Imperious* to rule the galaxy. Speaking as a poor, lowly Sapiens, might I say, 'fat chance.' Sire."

The Crown Prince shook his head. "You don't understand, Admiral. I am not talking the genocide of your species. Currently, *Homo Superior* are less than fifteen per cent of the total population. This is far too small a sampling to move the Empire forward.

"Over the next two thousand years, the Empire must continue to grow. As it does, the ratio of Superior to Sapiens will become balanced. Then the Superior will exceed the Sapiens. If the Sapiens are not prepared, then there will be a civil war which the Empire may not survive. As we have seen…" he waved his hand around…" Our enemies are not waiting. If we are at war with ourselves, we will surely fall."

"What does that have to do with the *Xian* and its victims?" Katy asked.

"The Sudahar have given us a mighty tool," he answered as he pulled the mind control spike from his pocket. "With this, we can be certain the Sapiens will stand with the Empire and not be co-opted to join our enemies."

"Gods below!" swore Doctor Ho-Bar. "You're talking about slavery."

"I'm talking about the survival of my Empire!" thundered the Heir. "Since I was conceived, my whole life's work had been for the good of my Empire. Your species is fading, though you can't see it now. When it becomes evident, what side would you be on, Doctor? With my Empire or with those who would destroy what we have all sworn to protect?"

"What of my role?" Katy asked. "You implied I have a role."

"Yes," the Heir said. "You will return to Terra for a year to acclimate to the High Command and, as a new Royal, learn the ways of the court. My mother wishes this. She has set a decree, so you are to live as Noyan-Behi, complete with staff and castle. Perhaps one near your childhood home, yes?"

"There are no castles near my childhood home," Katy responded, her voice careful and controlled.

"France then. Or any other part of Europa. After a year, you will be busy though, travelling from your home to my research facility on Maninquez. By then, we will have all these victims transferred there for care and research. You will command that facility."

"I am a Naval officer, Sire," Katy was struggling to keep control. "And I am a salvage officer. I hardly qualify to run a medical facility?"

"Who said anything about a medical facility?" asked the heir. "Maninquez is a research and development facility. What greater a salvage could you make, save the rescue of your own species?" He rose to his feet. "My fleet departs for Terra after your touching departure ceremony in seventy-two hours, Admiral. I expect you to join us after we honor the dead."

Crown Prince Abdul bin Russolov Khan, heir to the Throne of the Terran Empire, progenitor to the genus *Homo Imperious*, whirled and strode from the room. His second wife followed, stopping at the door. Her teeth flashed a broad grin. Laughing, she shadowed her husband.

Chapter 25

"'Tis a far, far better place I go, 'tis a far, far greater thing I do..." The words rattled around Katy's head. She wasn't drunk, not yet. The half bottle from a few weeks ago was empty, the one she'd been on when Ho-Bar threatened to stop her from the space jack mission. It tasted just as she remembered it, still the sticky caramel flavor with a hint of smoke, biting her belly and providing the much-needed kick. The glorious distortion between her temples was achingly familiar and so welcome. When her brain decided she'd had enough, it'd tell her to go lie down and sleep. The Glivenich would take care of any scary dreams she might have.

Ho-Bar could hardly object. He'd been on the ship of the Damned with her, sat in the room and listened to the Crown Prince's plan. The poor bastards weren't going to be rescued and joyously reunited with what remained of their families. No, they were to be herded off to the Empire's sickest research facility, test subjects for his mad plan to enslave the *Homo Sapiens*. And she was the cursed woman he chose to run the facility.

The good doctor had returned to *Mary Kane* with her. He followed Katy to her stateroom and took a long draft of the canvas covered bottle on her desk. Soon, that bottle was empty, and he started a second he had hidden in his bag. By the time the second bottle was nearly empty, he was falling asleep, muttering, "O.K. Katy. Two fingers! But that's all. Two fingerssss...."

A tap on the door. *Shave and a haircut...* "Enter Jhonny!" Katy called. His blond burr cut led the way as Captain Bosely poked his head and spied the unconscious doctor sleeping on the couch. "Should I call a soldier detachment to carry him to the shuttle?"

"Nah, leave him be. He only drank a bottle and a half. He'll be back to his asshole self in the morning," Katy enjoined.

Jhon pushed Ho-Bar's legs aside, sat, and held out a hand for the bottle. Gratefully, he drank.

"That bad, huh?" he asked.

"Worse," she said. "I'm to return to Terra with him and hole up in a castle for a year, learning to be the Noyan-Behi and Imperial war plans. Then I'm off to take charge of his death factory, finding new and creative ways to disable, dismember and kill. Starting with these thirty thousand, of course."

"Of course." Jhon took another long pull from the bottle. "Sounds like a good reason to have a drink or three."

"Yeah."

They sat passing the bottle until it emptied. Katy went to her locker and pulled out a second.

"See, the thing is, as I see it," Katy said as she pried the cork out with her teeth, spitting it across her stateroom, "is I'm damned if I do and I'm damned if I don't. If I follow his orders, the survivors go to Maninquez where they'll be tormented and tortured to death. If I don't follow his orders, I'll be strung up in the throne room for his pleasure and the thirty thousand will still go to Maninquez and die. I don't see any middle ground..." Her voice trailed off.

Jhon narrowed his eyes. "What are you thinking, Katy?"

"*Xian* is barely holding orbit now," she said. "It wouldn't take much to push him out of that orbit."

"No," Jhon acknowledged. "Two people in auxiliary control could pull it off. But where would you take him?"

"Back."

"Back where?"

"Back where we found him," she said. "If we hadn't found him when we did, we'd have never know he was there. He would have entered the photosphere and been destroyed. The Crown Prince couldn't stop *Xian*. Hell, we couldn't pull off the salvage of *Xian* a second time with the condition he's in."

John made an obvious point. "What about the pilot? The Crown Prince will skin him alive on the Plaza at Giza!"

"Yeah, there's that," Katy admitted. "Of course, if I just took *Xian* straight into the sun..."

"You can't be serious Katy," Jhon said. "Are you really suicidal or is that just the drink talking?"

"Jhon, it has to be me," she replied adamantly. "Anyone else and this Crown Prince blames me and takes it out on the fleet. If I succeed, maybe I piss him off enough where he lays all the blame on me and leaves the fleet alone. Either way, I'm just as dead. Burned alive in the Joeanmika star or skinned alive on the Plaza."

"Or I do nothing," she sighed. "And thirty thousand souls I swore an oath to protect die under my command."

They passed the bottle back and forth again, each taking a long draw. Jhon stood. "I'll go get your E.V.A. suit ready," he announced. "A shuttle would be too noticeable. I'll also contact Dan, have him pick an airlock to meet you. You'll need a second set of hands to control *Xian*. I suppose you'll ask Dan?"

"No, you'll need him here on *Mary Kane*." Katy said. "I think I already have a volunteer. As soon as I get on board, I'm going to order our people to quietly start to evacuate. Before I fire the engines, I'll set off the alarms and let the Imperials get off the best they can. I hope they get off in time, but I want to leave them as little time as possible."

"All right. See you in fifteen minutes?"

"Make it twenty," she said. I have to take care of a few things first."

Katy took her time to admire the universe for the last time as she made the hour-long transit from *Mary Kane* to *Xian*. Her home of the last twenty years faded into the universe as she accelerated away. *Mary Kane* was an ugly ship, all strange angles and lumps. Bare patches and painted repairs dotted his hull; the observer's pylon behind the bridge looked like it was stuck on him by a demented architect. His star drive bulged as the muscles of a vain bodybuilder, dwarfing the rest of the ship. The equipment sled was just strung behind the tug, covered with the tools and equipment that allowed the tug to do its work. He wasn't sleek and painted like the frigates and destroyers Katy had served on early in her career, more like the ratty and torn slippers she put on every evening because they fit just so.

Emotion surged as she watched her ship disappear. "Goodbye, old friend. Fare thee well," Katy whispered and turned back to her task, resolutely searching for *Xian*. Fifteen minutes out, a bright light in front of her began to elongate, eventually stretching into the recognizable form of the *Xian*. As she drew closer, she saw the scar left when brave Damari Russell saved the ship by towing the last five burning reactors free of the derelict. The ship was darker now, ominous. Katy shivered in spite of herself. Of course it was darker, there were no fires and Dan had cut power to most of the ship to save energy. Still, given the cargo, Katy swore she could hear ghoulies and goblins crawling through the ship.

A tiny strobing light flashed from the forward section of the engineering hull, opposite of the operational landing bay. Katy maneuvered her E.V.A. pack to the beacon and entered the airlock. "Hey Admiral, welcome aboard!" Diezac sounded cheerful, considering what she was about to do. "I have your volunteer." Gyona Philemon entered the airlock and helped Katy remove her helmet.

"Hello, Admiral," The bright eyes of the ancient Mykonon engineering glowed over her grey muzzle. "Dan said you needed help. Of course, since I know this ship better than he does, I volunteered immediately."

Katy removed her gloves and said, "I understood you were going home to Mykeros to take your last walk into the forest after

Taiho delivered the funeral sled to Terra. You must know this is a one-way mission. You will not survive to walk into your forest."

Gyona unfastened Katy's E.V.A. suit and helped her disrobe. "When Philemon was preparing to walk into the forest, he sat and spoke with his students one last time," she said. "There were many questions they wished to know about his journey while they still had time: 'Better to walk alone into the forest when it is your time than to wait even a minute for your friends to be ready,' he said. 'But if a dear friend is ready to make the walk and it is close to your time, then joyfully join your friend and walk together to the end.'"

Gyona continued as Katy donned her dress uniform. "You are making your walk into the forest, Katy," she said. "I am ready enough to make that walk with you. Come, let us take our final journey together, as friends."

Katy finished buttoning her blouse, then pulled on the sweater Grams had knitted her so long ago. It seemed more fitting, the familiar, comfortable cable knit wool from back home in Glanearagh. She hadn't thought of her old village back on Terra in decades, but now, just for a fleeting second, she wished she could be standing on the pier, watching for her father's fishing boat to return from the sea. Just one last time. She wrapped the sweater around herself, a hug from Grams, even years after she'd died.

Now she was preparing to walk to her own death, one way or another. Grams would approve of her friend Gyona. "Dan, evacuate our people immediately," she placed her hand on Gyona's shoulder. "We'll sound the general alarm when we're ready in Auxiliary

Control. I want our folks off of *Xian* and back on their own ships by then."

Two ways existed for movement through a ship the size of *Xian*. The easiest was to stroll down the hallways in a direct line to Auxiliary Control. The way would be lined by the Crown Prince's marines, who would doubtlessly report Katy's presence.

The other method was to utilize the hidden passages and tunnels used to maintain the ship. Gyona was certain the Imperial marines would be unaware of these passages. The engineers from the fleet would know of them. The Merkyonian hoped they wouldn't encounter any of the Imperials in the miles of tunnels.

Unobserved throughout their walk, a single marine guarded their destination. "Leave this to me," Gyona said, pulling a black plastic device from her pouch. The guard and Gyona argued for a moment before the marine acceded and opened the door, led Gyona into the chamber. Seconds later, Katy heard a sharp *crack-zzzzzz!* Gyona appeared at the door and waved.

Inside the door, the marine lay face down on the deck, a burn mark over his right kidney. "Silly engineers who designed this version of the battle suit ran too many conduits at this location of the armor," snorted Gyona. "Very susceptible to high voltage." She waved the hand stunner. "He's not dead, but his suit has locked up. He's not going anywhere."

Gyona dug a plasma torch from her bag and tossed it to Katy. "Weld the door shut, will you? I'll get started on the engine sequence programing. When I'm done, we'll switch places and you can input the navigation."

Katy hadn't welded in ten years and the door was thick blast molbydium, the bulkheads dynilom alloy. She worked slowly, carefully, ensuring her weld was solid and strong. A quarter of the way around the door, Gyona tapped her shoulder. "I'm done, Katy. Program the navigation while I finish the door."

Katy surrendered the torch and sat at the more familiar navigation station. *Xian's* computer was pernicious and slow, as though it understood Katy was programing the ship's demise. Undeterred, Katy created *Xian's* final course, the dive into the star. The computer protested several times, explaining over and over its objection to entering a solar mass. In the end, it reluctantly accepted Katy's instructions.

Gyona finished the door and assumed position at the engine controls. "Ready?" Katy asked. Gyona closed her eyes for a moment in prayer. "Ready, my friend. Shall we enter the forest now?"

Katy took a deep breath, set her jaw and resolutely pressed the general evacuation alarm. *Xian* began flashing red lights throughout the ship and its loud male voice announced, "Attention! This is a disaster alert. The ship is set for self-destruct. All personnel are to evacuate immediately!" The announcement repeated itself over and over. Katy initiated the navigation program, then counted down, "Engines in three…two…one…Engines, full power!"

Xian lurched and shook; loud groans and snaps exploded throughout the ship as the remaining drive, supplemented by the assist power units that had been attached weeks ago when *Xian* was lifted into this orbit. Console after console in the control room arced and exploded, adding to the confusion. But, for all its protestations, *Xian* was responding on course and speed. The ship would enter the photosphere of Joeanmika star in two standard hours.

"Auxiliary Control! This is the Crown Prince. Respond please!"

Katy pressed her palms over her eyes. She hadn't thought the Crown Prince would be aboard, complicating her plan. Momentarily, Katy wished she had a god to look to for guidance, such as Gyona had.

Damnit, she'd just have to wing it.

"Majesty, this is Admiral O'Hare onboard *Xian*," she called. "Sir, I regret to report *Xian* has been sabotaged! Engineer Gyona and I here trying to override the programing, but we have found extensive damage in Auxiliary Control. I fear the ship is unrecoverable. I have sounded the evacuation alarm and recommend you order your officers and ratings evacuate at once."

"I am five minutes away, Admiral," the Crown Prince said. "I have an engineering team with me. We'll get that door open, Katy, then see what can be done."

"Highness, I implore you," Katy said. "*Xian* is accelerating. Engineer Gyona and I will find the solution. But you must evacuate immediately. Sire, you are too important to the Empire to die in this fashion. Please, Sire."

Gyona and Katy began smashing the remaining consoles. Each time a console was struck, a brilliant cascade of sparks exploded from the panel. The smell of ozone and smoke filled the room.

"Admiral, this is Gunnery Sergeant Gerald Stillings, Imperial Marines," a strong voice announced through the comm. "I am outside Auxiliary Control with my sapper unit and the repair team. Ma'am, can you open the doors, please?"

"We've tried, Gunnery Sergeant," Katy answered. "They are quite jammed. I insist you and your teams evacuate immediately."

"No can do, Ma'am," Stillings responded. "The Crown Prince has ordered me to rescue you. The repair team is to salvage *Xian*."

"Sergeant, I order you to evacuate your team," Katy said.

The Heir's voice was commanding. "Katy, this is the Crown Prince. I appreciate your courage in the face of this crisis. I am outside now, supervising your rescue. Patience, my friend. We will have the door open momentarily."

"Admiral, the door appears to be mechanically frozen," reported Sergeant Stillings. "We're going to rig it with explosives. Ma'am, I will need you and your companion to find a safe location in the room. Perpendicular to the door would be best, but certainly behind any solid object within the room. We'll be ready in two minutes."

Two minutes. The whole of her life was to be wrapped up in two minutes. Gyona took Katy's hand and led her in front of the door. "I am ready to take my walk now, Katy," she said, squeezing the Terran woman's hand.

"As am I," was Katy's hesitant reply.

"Just another minute, Admiral," Stillings reported. "Have you found refuge?"

"We have, Sergeant."

Gyona squeezed Katy's hand. "I am glad you are walking into the forest with me, Katy."

"Thirty seconds."

"I fear I am afraid, Gyona," Katy ventured.

"I am here, Katy," Gyona wrapped her arm around Katy's. "I will be with you until the end. Close your eyes. Can you see it? The forest is so beautiful today."

"Ten seconds."

Katy closed her eyes. She was back in the forest on Vespa with Andre. He was standing there, his hand reaching to hers, his smile as dazzling as a nova.

"Five…four…three…"

Katy took Andre's outstretched hand and leaned towards him for a kiss…

"One."

The blast was deafening.

Chapter 26

A hammer blow struck Katy across her entire body. She expected the explosion and the door's impact on her body to kill her on the spot. To her dismay, she remained conscious while she collided with the wall, the door and shock wave crushing her against the bulkhead. An aborted yelp was the single sound from Gyona.

Katy's body was squashed. She could feel bones splinter, internal organs rupture. She was stunned, not just from the impact, but because she was still alive. The heavy door hadn't bounced; Katy and Gyona's bodies had absorbed the inertia. Katy's head hung on the top lip of the twisted, shattered door. Gyona's lifeless hand was still in hers.

Why was she still alive? Where was the pain? She should be in agonizing pain.

Then she gasped. There it was. The pain. Her body must have been so shocked that the agony took seconds to start. She tried to draw a breath, ruined lungs scraping against shattered ribs. "Ghaaaa…" she croaked, for the pain was intolerable.

The Marines entered the smoky chamber. One dashed to the door and tried to lift it. Katy cried out, so he set it down, screaming, "Corpsman!"

Crown Prince Abdul bin Russolov strode into the room, the repair team following him through the ruined door and scattering around the devastated control room. He knelt next to Katy and placed his hand behind her head. "Oh, Katy, what have you done?" he asked, his voice calm and soothing. "You were told to seek shelter; why did you stand in front of the door?"

Katy tried to answer, but her words were lost in a moan as another wave of agony flowed through her. A small, tender mercy arrived; she could no longer feel her legs. Hot tears flowed from her eyes; she tasted coppery blood in her mouth. Attempting to explain herself to the Heir was agonizing; she could only groan. Another inhalation and shattered ribs tore at her.

It is taking too long to die.

The corpsman appeared, tore open his bag and injected Katy with a painkiller. Alas, his medication stood no chance against the recurring onslaught of Katy's suffering. Still, she began to experience less and less agony as her tormented nervous system began to shut down. The corpsman waved a medical scanner over Katy, its searching beams easily penetrating the heavy door that crushed her. He looked to the Crown Prince and shook his head slightly.

"Majesty!" came a cry. An engineer saluted and stated, "Sire, the controls, they're all smashed."

"Can you repair them?"

"Given time, yes, Sir," said the engineer. "But as near as I can tell, the engines and power units are on full thrust. Navigation is indicating the course is locked. This ship is headed straight for the sun."

"What? How?" The Crown Prince was, confused. "How, Admiral? Why is this happening?"

Katy actually smiled, a blood-stained grimace. She mustered what strength she had and whispered, "I had to, you see? I had to keep them out of your grasp..." The effort exhausted her, and she struggled to breathe, managing only a weak, panting gasp.

"You bitch!" he screamed. "Traitor! Look at all I gave you, all I was going to give you, and you betrayed me!" He kicked at the fallen door, moving it naught but eliciting another groan from the dying Admiral.

"How fortunate you have no family," he hissed. "They would be made to suffer for your treason. I wonder, how far does this treachery go? Your ship, your precious *Mary Kane*. Yes, that's where I'll start." He whirled around and stalked to the door. He stopped and called, "Sergeant Stillings!"

"Yes, Majesty?"

"Execute this traitor. Then see to it all my troops and engineers are evacuated as well," the Crown Prince ordered. "Any Terran found who not part of my Battle Fleet is considered part of Admiral O'Hare's conspiracy and is to be executed on the spot." He stormed away.

Gunnery Sergeant Stillings pulled out his sidearm, a short-ranged pulse laser. He aimed it at the traitor's head, though he knew the woman would be dead in minutes anyway. Well, orders were orders.

Katy stared up the muzzle of the weapon. The emitter crystal glowed a cheery red.

"Oh, how pretty!"

"Mary Kane! Mary Kane! This is shuttle MK01! Prepare for emergency docking! This is Dan Diezac. Get me Captain Bosley on line, immediately!" The normally staid engineer sounded on the verge of panic.

"Shuttle MK01, this is *Mary Kane* actual. It's me, Danny," Jhon Bosley reported. "Shuttle dock is ready. What's happened?"

"She's dead, Jhon," Dan sobbed. "That fracking Crown Prince had Katy killed. She set the *Xian* on course for the star. He declared her a traitor and had her killed. Gods below, Jhon, we've got to get out of here! He's ordered the *Mary Kane* taken; we're all going to be deep scanned by Imperial Intelligence."

"I know, Dan," Jhon said. "So did Katy. Dock immediately, then get your arse to engineering. We're getting out of here, the whole fleet."

"Wilco. Three minutes."

Jhon Bosley snapped, "Salvage Fleet on comm, now!" When the young officer nodded, Jhon announced, "Attention, First Salvage Fleet of the Terran Empire. Admiral O'Hare is dead. The Crown Prince has declared her a traitor and all of us conspirators. Execute contingency P'Ger-sa one-nine. Captain/Sister 93 launch all fighters to cover the fleet's withdrawal, but do not fire unless fired upon.

These are Imperial ships pursuing us and I refuse to start an internecine battle with my own countrymen."

The tall, yellow-green Vinithri appeared in the holo tank. "The honor is to serve," came the translation. "In this world and the next. *Victory* will give you time to escape. Farewell." She raised a leg as the holo faded.

Doctor Ho-Bar entered the bridge. "Jhon, what's happening?"

"Tactical," ordered Jhon. The system map popped up, showing the salvage fleet ships twisting about, delayed by picking up space jacks and cutters. The fleet's frigates moved into position between the Battle Fleet and the Salvage. They would be cut to ribbons in seconds, Jhon knew. But they all had sworn their lives to Katy in life, and each would sacrifice theirs for her in death.

Ho-Bar staggered, gripping a chair to hold himself up. "I have to return to *Tranquility,*" he said.

"No time," barked Jhon, "Everyone is headed for the rendezvous point. We can transfer you there."

"But my ship," begged the Doctor.

"Right now, I'm trying to save my own," snapped Captain Bosley. "Stay out of the way."

"Green lights," came the call from the aft bridge. "The ship is programed for the jump."

"Is Diezac's shuttle aboard yet?"

"Docking now, Sir."

"As soon as he's aboard, jettison the work sled," ordered the Captain. "Deploy the jump tachyon guides, start the countdown." Long antennae, like a cat's whiskers, deployed from the bow of the ship. A low thrumb was both felt and heard throughout the tug as the tachyon capacitors began to charge.

"*Mary Kane*, this is *Loki*. By order of the Crown Prince, I order you to stand down and heave to." Tan's image filled the holo tank. "This is Intelligence Master Tan sa-Khan. You will comply. Shut down your engines immediately and prepare to be boarded."

Jhon Bosley stood straight. "*Loki*, this is *Mary Kane*. Tan, it's me, Jhon Bosley. You know this is illegal. Your Crown Prince cannot order an Imperial vessel to halt and allow your agents to scan any of us. It flies right into the Laws of Privacy. We are departing this location, the entire fleet. We will rendezvous with you at Terra."

"You are trying to quote the Laws of my Grandfather to me?" Tan asked. "I will not be contradicted by a *Sapiens*. Heave to immediately or suffer the consequences."

"Diezac is aboard, sir, jettisoning the sled." *Mary Kane* jolted, and the helmsman instantly increased the thrust. *Mary Kane* raced away from the advancing *Loki*, rattling and shaking with the power surge. "*Loki* is firing," came the report. "Negligible damage. Distance from *Loki* increasing."

"We have more thrust available," said Captain Bosley. "Start the jump sequence; give me tactical on the holo."

The holo displayed the local system. The scattered ships had collected their space jacks and cutters; the scouts had already departed for the rally point. *Victory's* forty fighters were positioning themselves between their charges and the Battle Fleet. Already, green symbols of *Victory's* fighters were breaking into clouds of dust, along with the blue symbols of the Battle Fleets fighters. *A lot of loyal beings are dying today,* mused Jhon Bosley sadly.

A cluster of three blue symbols closed on *Repose*. "Gods below, NO!" Jhon screamed. "Get me that group! Those are heroes they're attack…" The blue symbols shifted to an attack pattern, the holographic symbol of the mortuary ship dissolved into dozens of pieces.

Mary Kane shook again, more violently. "Captain look!" came the cry.

Ashira was on an intercept course with *Mary Kane*.

The ship shook yet again. The dull throb of the jump capacitors was suddenly silent. "Sir, we've lost the starboard Tachyon emitter," reported a young officer. Bosley looked to the display again, desperately. They couldn't outrun *Ashira*. *Mary Kane* was grossly outgunned. Much of his fleet had escaped, he noted. But six clouds of green symbols showed not everyone was getting away. A seventh, *Victory,* was ringed in red, revealing he was battered and dying, blue wedges of fighters, frigates and a lone destroyer devastating the fleet carrier. Moments later, *Victory* was shattered.

"Show me the *Ashira*," Jhon ordered. The onrushing Command Battle Carrier was closing. At a flash from its prow, the *Mary Kane's* helmsman dodged and ducked. The ship was slammed from the stern, pitching nose down and tumbling. Frames groaned, lights and panels exploded as the *Mary Kane* tumbled. There were cries of fear as the bridge filled with smoke. "Stabilize my ship," roared Captain Bosley. "Damage reports!"

The helmsman struggled and righted the ship. "Engineering here," came Diezac's voice.

"Tell me some good news, Dan," Bosley asked.

"None sir," responded the engineer. "That last shot tore off the dorsal star drive. Computer has shut down into default mode. Worse of all, the inertial dampeners are spinning down. You've got two, maybe three more turns before they're ineffective."

News of the inertial dampeners chilled Jhon's blood. Even moving at *.1 c* required the dampeners, less the fragile human crew be slammed against the nearest bulkhead during any maneuver. The ancient Laws of Newton. With no dampeners, he couldn't even stop the ship to surrender. Oh, he could let it drift to a stop; that should take at this speed…two standard years.

Two, maybe three more turns. He called for tactical again. *Ashira*, recognizing *Mary Kane* was crippled, was taking a wide, lazy orbit to get back into a firing position.

He spied a white series of symbols, in a lower orbit. "There!" he pointed, "One turn, put us there."

"The reactors?" puzzled the helmsman, also spotting the reactors jettisoned from the doomed *Xian*.

"The radiation they're spewing will be enough to mask us from their sensors," Jhon explained. "Perhaps we can get the inertial dampeners and Tachyon emitters repaired sufficiently to escape."

"Might work," called Diezac. "I'll need twenty-four hours for the dampeners, considerably less for the emitters. The spare emitter is secured to the hull, so a crew of space jacks can have that swapped out in an hour."

"That much radiation will limit each space jack to less than ten minutes," Ho-Bar said. "You'll need me in medical to see if we can save them."

"Do it," ordered Captain Jhon Bosley. *Katy, watch over us this one last time,* he prayed.

Crown Prince Abdul bin Russolov ne-Khan studied the crippled tug *Mary Kane* as it made the turn and began to maneuver away. While he admired the plucky nature in which this Captain had fought his ship, indeed his entire fleet, the Heir was getting bored. At least the Vinithri had shown proper respect, messaging her farewell to the Crown Prince before his ships destroyed her vessel.

He ordered the tactical display up. Ah, the course of the little tug was clear. This Captain was risking taking his ship amongst the burning reactors from the *Xian,* perhaps hoping the radiation would shield him enough to effect repairs and escape. Had he been against a *Sapiens* opponent, the tactic might very well have worked. Poor

Sapiens, his opponent this day was a member of the *Homo Superiors.* While brave, the tactic was easily discerned with his superior intellect. He ordered the meson weapons to full charge and targeted on the reactor debris field.

The radiation alarms screamed in every compartment onboard *Mary Kane.* Captain Bosley ordered them shut down on his bridge. Frustratingly, as soon as it was turned off, the alarm would start its wailing again. Finally, an armed guard shot the comm speaker off the wall.

Doctor Ho-Bar rushed down to the medical suite. Already running through his mind were the protocols for high level radiation burns. He began to plan his triage.

Dan Diezac had pulled the power from the primary inertial dampener. When they lifted the cover, Dan saw that one arm holding the twenty nuetronium weights was bent and the raceway in the spin chamber had been gouged by the errant weight. An easier fix than he had anticipated. Pull the rotating mass, have a new arm manufactured in the machine shop and reinstalled. Meanwhile, he'd enter the primary chamber, smooth out the damage and re-polish the entire chamber. It wouldn't be perfect, but at least they might make the rendezvous on time. He called for the tools to start removing the rotating mass.

Two space jacks clomped along the hull of the *Mary Kane* to the spare emitter antennae. Another pair were at the sheared-off machinery. Six bolts, that was all, and a pair of wiring plugs.

They'd have the old emitter off in minutes, the new one in place in an hour. Then a seven-day sleep in the regen tanks and heroes when they emerged!

The space jacks could easily look up and barely make out the glowing predator, *Ashira*. The Captain had said the debris field of the reactors from the *Xian* would shield and protect them from the Imperial flagship. It was unnerving to see the enemy so close. Still, Captain Bosley was Admiral O'Hare's handpicked successor. Surely, he'd know just what to do.

A second before they died, one space jack noticed a flash at *Ashira's* bow…

The primary weapon on most Imperial ships was the meson rifle. Microscopic particle mass was spun up and released down reflective barrels at light speed. The reflective barrels themselves were rifled, ensuring each shot stayed compact and focused onto target.

The size of the particles was inconsequential. The mass moved at the speed of light. As Bosley turned to admonish the shooter, between Ho-Bar's steps to medical, as Diezac reached for a wrench, a septillion of microscopic crystals tore through *Mary Kane* so rapidly that the energy release barely resembled an explosion. One moment, the ship was coasting amongst the rubble they believed their refuge, the next *Mary Kane* was a cloud of free falling dust.

Too fast to even to register they had all died.

Abdul and Tan ate their supper in the grand chamber of the Khan aboard *Ashira*.

"You have no regrets at the deaths of your friends, Tan?" he asked.

"None, Husband. You may scan me and see this is so. They were, after all, simple *Sapiens*. Still, what are we to tell your mother?"

The Crown Prince frowned. The *Sapiens* Admiral and traitor, Katy O'Hare, had been a favorite of his mother's, after all. She would not be pleased should she learn what happen at the Joeanmika system. He had not yet accumulated enough power to challenge her…yet. So, they would need an airtight alibi.

"The ships that escaped," he asked. "You have agents aboard?"

"Yes. All are Superior, so when the enemy comes out at their rendezvous point, it will be easy enough to incapacitate the Terran crew. As well as most of the aliens. Those who are not susceptible to our talents will be easily enough subdued," she told him.

"So, while salvaging the ships from the battle at Joeanmika system, Imperial Salvage Fleet One was set upon by a savage group of pirates. Better still, a new race, the Feloids and their allies, the Sudahar. Our Fleet fought bravely, but the enemy was too great. Sadly, there were no survivors," he stated. "Save, of course, the ones we transport to Maninquez. Granted, not the thirty thousand we planned for. But these are healthy specimens, they will provide better data." He raised his wine glass. "Salute, to the brave soldiers of the late First Salvage fleet."

"And brave Admiral Katy O'Hare who fought with her hands on the controls of her own ship, dying only after all hope was lost." Tan extended herself into Abdul's head, gently stroking the passion center of her husband. She could feel him responding. *He may be* Superior, she mused, *but I know how to convince my husband to get what I want.* "Any other description will only make your mother suspicious. We are not yet strong enough to confront her. In another year, perhaps. For now, we must discuss the elimination of your first wife and her inferior children…"

The Ballad of Katy O'Hare: Epilog

Inhale. Pain!

Exhale. Agony!

Nothing had changed. He was sure. All current memory was a life of pain. He clung to what he could remember of the time before. A distant memory of the sun, the fields of grain. His wife. His children.

The device punished him for the memories. His wife, dead, torn to pieces by the giant cats. His sons, dead, one slashed and torn by the enemy, the other who allowed himself to be infected and died at the hands of the Other's slaves. His daughters wrapped in cocoons and carried away. It would show his family dying over and over while stimulating his pain centers.

A being in black was before him. He allowed himself hope as it touched his mind. "Are you there?" it asked. "Can you tell me your name, your world?" He screamed his name over the shards of pain the device tormented him with. He begged to know the fate of his daughters.

The being left. Torment continued.

He couldn't survive this much longer. Time was marked only by the forced feedings and cleanings by the blue shorted slaves. The device would laugh at him when he begged for death.

An extraordinary day! A being in gold was before him. It asked his name in a soothing voice. He screamed his name and begged to know the fate of his daughters. The being smiled and patted his cheek. "Have courage, young Lars," it had said. "I promise you we'll find your daughters and return them to you."

The old woman, in a blue uniform searched his face for answers. "My daughters, please?" he begged. The device laughed again and stabbed agony deep into his core. She turned and departed with the others.

What was happening? The ship rattled and groaned, rolling side to side. Horrid noises rang all around him. Red lights flashed as he swayed in reaction to the gyrations of the ship. An announcement to evacuate the ship. Black humor, the ship that held him captive and punished him for untold sins was to be abandoned, leaving him and his fellow captives behind again. Crowds of beings hurried past, paying no attention to his screaming.

Back to the timeless punishment. Inhale. Pain! Exhale. Agony! The ship continued to rattle and shake, and he could hear distant explosions. A roar grew louder and louder in his ears.

A ship-shattering shake and the mountings that held him to the walls snapped. He cried as his body landed heavily on the deck. The others around him had been tossed to the floor as well, a pile of the tormented, dying men. The walls were collapsing around them, he saw, and it was becoming harder to breath. The device in his head was confused, now seemingly forgetting to punish him. The temperature grew hotter and hotter; he felt his own weight growing heavier and heavier. It was a futile struggle to breathe the blistering air.

The other in his head gave an electronic scream and fled. He heard the roaring behind him, felt the fires that burned the ship begin to lick at his back. Lars cried out with joy, they were there, his family, before him! Mara, the love of his life, whole and as beautiful as when he first met her. His four sons, strong and proud. The two jewels of his life, the daughters he had prayed to see once last time. "Come on, Da!" Mika cried. "It's time to go, Da!" cried Mila, tugging his arm.

The air around them flashed tongues of fire as its gases added to the holocaust. Lars Thomas inhaled deeply, purposefully, and surrendered himself to outstretched arms. "Beloveds," he sighed with a last Xian breath. "I'm home."

Made in the USA
Columbia, SC
05 July 2018